www.EffortlessMath.com

... So Much More Online!

✓ FREE Math lessons

✓ More Math learning books!

✓ Mathematics Worksheets

✓ Online Math Tutors

Need a PDF version of this book?

Please visit www.EffortlessMath.com

SHSAT Math Study Guide 2020 - 2021

A Comprehensive Review and Step-By-Step Guide to Preparing for the SHSAT Math

By

Reza Nazari & Ava Ross

All inquiries should be addressed to:

info@effortlessMath.com

www.EffortlessMath.com

ISBN: 978-1-64612-303-2

Published by: Effortless Math Education

www.EffortlessMath.com

Visit www.EffortlessMath.com

for Online Math Practice

Description

SHSAT Math Study Guide, which reflects the 2020 - 2021 test guidelines, is designed by top SHSAT Math instructors and test prep experts to help test takers succeed on the SHSAT Math Test. The updated version of this comprehensive SHSAT Math preparation book includes Math lessons, extensive exercises, sample SHSAT Math questions, and quizzes with answers and detailed solutions to help you hone your math skills, overcome your exam anxiety, boost your confidence—and do your best to ace the SHSAT exam on test day. Upon completion of this perfect SHSAT Math prep book, you will have a solid foundation and sufficient practice to ace the SHSAT Math test.

Not only does this all-inclusive prep book offer everything you will ever need to prepare for the SHSAT Math test, but it also contains two complete and realistic SHSAT Math tests that reflect the format and question types on the SHSAT to help you check your exam-readiness and identify where you need more practice.

SHSAT Math Study Guide contains many exciting and unique features to help you prepare for the SHSAT Math test, including:

- ✓ Content 100% aligned with the 2020 SHSAT® test
- ✓ Written by SHSAT Math instructors and test experts
- ✓ Complete coverage of all SHSAT Math concepts and topics which you will be tested
- ✓ Step-by-step guide for all SHSAT Math topics
- ✓ Abundant Math skill building exercises to help test-takers approach different question types that might be unfamiliar to them
- ✓ Exercises on different SHSAT Math topics such as integers, percent, equations, polynomials, exponents and radicals
- ✓ 2 full-length practice tests (featuring new question types) with detailed answers

This SHSAT Math prep book and other Effortless Math Education books are used by thousands of students each year to help them review core content areas, brush-up in math, discover their strengths and weaknesses, and achieve their best scores on the SHSAT test.

Contents

Description 1

Simplifying Fractions 6

Adding and Subtracting Fractions 8

Multiplying and Dividing Fractions 10

Adding Mixed Numbers 12

Subtracting Mixed Numbers 14

Multiplying Mixed Numbers 16

Dividing Mixed Numbers 18

Comparing Decimals 20

Rounding Decimals 22

Adding and Subtracting Decimals 24

Multiplying and Dividing Decimals 26

Adding and Subtracting Integers 28

Multiplying and Dividing Integers 30

Order of Operation 32

Integers and Absolute Value 34

Simplifying Ratios 36

Proportional Ratios 38

Create Proportion 40

Similarity and Ratios 42

Percent Problems 44

Percent of Increase and Decrease 46

Discount, Tax and Tip 48

Simple Interest 50

Simplifying Variable Expressions 52

Simplifying Polynomial Expressions 54

Evaluating One Variable 56

Evaluating Two Variables 58

The Distributive Property 60

One–Step Equations 62

System of Equations 66

Graphing Single–Variable Inequalities 68

One–Step Inequalities 70

Multi –Step Inequalities 72

Finding Slope 74

Graphing Lines Using Slope–Intercept Form 76

Writing Linear Equations 78

Finding Midpoint 80

Finding Distance of Two Points 82

Multiplication Property of Exponents 84

Division Property of Exponents 86

Powers of Products and Quotients 88

Zero and Negative Exponents 90

Negative Exponents and Negative Bases 92

Scientific Notation 94

Radicals 96

Simplifying Polynomials 98

Adding and Subtracting Polynomials 100

Multiplying Binomials 102

Multiplying and Dividing Monomials 104

Multiplying a Polynomial and a Monomial 106

Multiplying Monomials 108

Factoring Trinomials 110

The Pythagorean Theorem 112

Triangles 114

Polygons 116

Circles 118

Cubes 120

Trapezoids 122

Rectangular Prisms 124

Cylinder 126

Mean, Median, Mode, and Range of the Given Data 128

Probability Problems 130

www.EffortlessMath.com

Pie Graph..132

Permutations and Combinations 134

Function Notation and Evaluation 136

Adding and Subtracting Functions 138

Multiplying and Dividing Functions..140

Composition of Functions 142

SHSAT Test Review...144

SHSAT Mathematics Practice Test 1 150

SHSAT Mathematics Practice Test 2 167

SHSAT Mathematics Practice Tests Answers and Explanations........................184

Name:	Date: ....

Topic	Simplifying Fractions	
Notes	✓ Evenly divide both the top and bottom of the fraction by $2, 3, 5, 7, \ldots$ etc. ✓ Continue until you can't go any further.	
Example	*Simplify* $\frac{36}{48}$ To simplify $\frac{36}{48}$, find a number that both 36 and 48 are divisible by. Both are divisible by 12. Then: $\frac{36}{48} = \frac{36 \div 12}{48 \div 12} = \frac{3}{4}$	
Your Turn!	1) $\frac{2}{18} =$	2) $\frac{22}{66} =$
	3) $\frac{12}{48} =$	4) $\frac{11}{99} =$
	5) $\frac{15}{75} =$	6) $\frac{25}{100} =$
	7) $\frac{16}{72} =$	8) $\frac{32}{96} =$
	9) $\frac{14}{77} =$	10) $\frac{60}{84} =$

Name:	Date: ....

Topic	**Simplifying Fractions - Answers**	
Notes	✓ Evenly divide both the top and bottom of the fraction by $2, 3, 5, 7, \dots$ etc. ✓ Continue until you can't go any further.	
Example	**Simplify** $\frac{36}{48}$ To simplify $\frac{36}{48}$, find a number that both 36 and 48 are divisible by. Both are divisible by 12. Then: $\frac{36}{48} = \frac{36 \div 12}{48 \div 12} = \frac{3}{4}$	
Your Turn!	1) $\frac{2}{18} = \frac{1}{9}$	2) $\frac{22}{66} = \frac{1}{3}$
	3) $\frac{12}{48} = \frac{1}{4}$	4) $\frac{11}{99} = \frac{1}{9}$
	5) $\frac{15}{75} = \frac{1}{5}$	6) $\frac{25}{100} = \frac{1}{4}$
	7) $\frac{16}{72} = \frac{2}{9}$	8) $\frac{32}{96} = \frac{1}{3}$
	9) $\frac{14}{77} = \frac{2}{11}$	10) $\frac{60}{84} = \frac{5}{7}$

Name:	Date: ....

Topic	**Adding and Subtracting Fractions**	
Notes	✓ For "like" fractions (fractions with the same denominator), add or subtract the numerators and write the answer over the common denominator. ✓ Find equivalent fractions with the same denominator before you can add or subtract fractions with different denominators. ✓ Adding and Subtracting with the same denominator: $$\frac{a}{b} + \frac{c}{b} = \frac{a+c}{b} \ , \frac{a}{b} - \frac{c}{b} = \frac{a-c}{b}$$ ✓ Adding and Subtracting fractions with different denominators: $$\frac{a}{b} + \frac{c}{d} = \frac{ad+bc}{bd} , \frac{a}{b} - \frac{c}{d} = \frac{ad-bc}{bd}$$	
Example	***Find the sum.*** $\frac{3}{5} + \frac{2}{3} = \frac{(3)3+(5)(2)}{5 \times 3} = \frac{19}{15}$ ***Subtract.*** $\frac{4}{7} - \frac{3}{7} = \frac{1}{7}$	
Your Turn!	1) $\frac{3}{5} + \frac{2}{7} =$	2) $\frac{7}{9} - \frac{4}{7} =$
	3) $\frac{4}{9} + \frac{5}{8} =$	4) $\frac{5}{8} - \frac{2}{5} =$
	5) $\frac{2}{5} + \frac{1}{6} =$	6) $\frac{2}{3} - \frac{1}{4} =$
	7) $\frac{8}{9} + \frac{5}{7} =$	8) $\frac{6}{7} - \frac{5}{9} =$

Name:	Date: ....

Topic	Adding and Subtracting Fractions - Answers
Notes	✓ For "like" fractions (fractions with the same denominator), add or subtract the numerators and write the answer over the common denominator. ✓ Find equivalent fractions with the same denominator before you can add or subtract fractions with different denominators. ✓ Adding and Subtracting with the same denominator: $$\frac{a}{b} + \frac{c}{b} = \frac{a+c}{b}, \quad \frac{a}{b} - \frac{c}{b} = \frac{a-c}{b}$$ ✓ Adding and Subtracting fractions with different denominators: $$\frac{a}{b} + \frac{c}{d} = \frac{ad+bc}{bd}, \frac{a}{b} - \frac{c}{d} = \frac{ad-bc}{bd}$$
Example	**Find the sum.** $\frac{3}{5} + \frac{2}{3} = \frac{(3)3+(5)(2)}{5 \times 3} = \frac{19}{15}$ **Subtract.** $\frac{4}{7} - \frac{3}{7} = \frac{1}{7}$
Your Turn!	1) $\frac{3}{5} + \frac{2}{7} = \frac{31}{35}$ 2) $\frac{7}{9} - \frac{4}{7} = \frac{13}{63}$ 3) $\frac{4}{9} + \frac{5}{8} = \frac{77}{72}$ 4) $\frac{5}{8} - \frac{2}{5} = \frac{9}{40}$ 5) $\frac{2}{5} + \frac{1}{6} = \frac{17}{30}$ 6) $\frac{2}{3} - \frac{1}{4} = \frac{5}{12}$ 7) $\frac{8}{9} + \frac{5}{7} = \frac{101}{63}$ 8) $\frac{6}{7} - \frac{5}{9} = \frac{19}{63}$

Name:	Date: ....

Topic	**Multiplying and Dividing Fractions**
Notes	✓ Multiplying fractions: multiply the top numbers and multiply the bottom numbers. ✓ Dividing fractions: Keep, Change, Flip Keep first fraction, change division sign to multiplication, and flip the numerator and denominator of the second fraction. Then, solve!
Examples	*Multiply.* $\frac{2}{5} \times \frac{3}{4} =$ Multiply the top numbers and multiply the bottom numbers. $\frac{2}{5} \times \frac{3}{4} = \frac{2\times3}{5\times4} = \frac{6}{20}$, simplify: $\frac{6}{2} = \frac{6\div2}{20\div2} = \frac{3}{10}$ *Divide.* $\frac{2}{5} \div \frac{3}{4} =$ Keep first fraction, change division sign to multiplication, and flip the numerator and denominator of the second fraction. Then: $\frac{2}{5} \div \frac{3}{4} = \frac{2}{5} \times \frac{4}{3} = \frac{2\times4}{5\times3} = \frac{8}{15}$
Your Turn!	1) $\frac{5}{9} \times \frac{4}{7} =$ 2) $\frac{3}{5} \div \frac{2}{3} =$ 3) $\frac{2}{7} \times \frac{3}{5} =$ 4) $\frac{2}{5} \div \frac{7}{12} =$ 5) $\frac{1}{7} \times \frac{4}{9} =$ 6) $\frac{2}{9} \div \frac{3}{7} =$ 7) $\frac{2}{5} \times \frac{6}{7} =$ 8) $\frac{1}{4} \div \frac{2}{5} =$

| Name: .... | Date: .... |

Topic	**Multiplying and Dividing Fractions - Answers**
Notes	✓ Multiplying fractions: multiply the top numbers and multiply the bottom numbers. ✓ Dividing fractions: Keep, Change, Flip Keep first fraction, change division sign to multiplication, and flip the numerator and denominator of the second fraction. Then, solve!
Examples	***Multiply.*** $\frac{2}{5} \times \frac{3}{4} =$ Multiply the top numbers and multiply the bottom numbers. $\frac{2}{5} \times \frac{3}{4} = \frac{2\times3}{5\times4} = \frac{6}{20}$, simplify: $\frac{6}{2} = \frac{6\div2}{20\div2} = \frac{3}{10}$ ***Divide.*** $\frac{2}{5} \div \frac{3}{4} =$ Keep first fraction, change division sign to multiplication, and flip the numerator and denominator of the second fraction. Then: $\frac{2}{5} \div \frac{3}{4} = \frac{2}{5} \times \frac{4}{3} = \frac{2\times4}{5\times3} = \frac{8}{15}$

Your Turn!	1) $\frac{5}{9} \times \frac{4}{7} = \frac{20}{63}$	2) $\frac{3}{5} \div \frac{2}{3} = \frac{9}{10}$
	3) $\frac{2}{7} \times \frac{3}{5} = \frac{6}{35}$	4) $\frac{2}{5} \div \frac{7}{12} = \frac{24}{35}$
	5) $\frac{1}{7} \times \frac{4}{9} = \frac{4}{63}$	6) $\frac{2}{9} \div \frac{3}{7} = \frac{14}{27}$
	7) $\frac{2}{5} \times \frac{6}{7} = \frac{12}{35}$	8) $\frac{1}{4} \div \frac{2}{5} = \frac{5}{8}$

Name: .... **Date:** ....

Topic	Adding Mixed Numbers	
Notes	Use the following steps for adding mixed numbers. ✓ Add whole numbers of the mixed numbers. ✓ Add the fractions of each mixed number. ✓ Find the Least Common Denominator (LCD) if necessary. ✓ Add whole numbers and fractions. ✓ Write your answer in lowest terms.	
Example	***Add mixed numbers.*** $1\frac{1}{2} + 2\frac{2}{3} =$ Rewriting our equation with parts separated, $1 + \frac{1}{2} + 2 + \frac{2}{3}$ Add whole numbers: $1 + 2 = 3$ Add fractions: $\frac{1}{2} + \frac{2}{3} = \frac{3}{6} + \frac{4}{6} = \frac{7}{6} = 1\frac{1}{6}$, Now, combine the whole and fraction parts: $3 + 1 + \frac{1}{6} = 4\frac{1}{6}$	
Your Turn!	1) $1\frac{1}{12} + 2\frac{3}{4} =$ 3) $1\frac{1}{10} + 2\frac{2}{5} =$ 5) $2\frac{2}{7} + 1\frac{2}{21} =$ 7) $3\frac{1}{5} + 1\frac{2}{8} =$	2) $3\frac{5}{8} + 1\frac{1}{4} =$ 4) $2\frac{5}{6} + 2\frac{2}{9} =$ 6) $1\frac{3}{8} + 3\frac{2}{3} =$ 8) $3\frac{1}{2} + 2\frac{3}{7} =$

Name:	Date: ....

Topic	**Adding Mixed Numbers - Answers**
Notes	Use the following steps for adding mixed numbers. ✓ Add whole numbers of the mixed numbers. ✓ Add the fractions of each mixed number. ✓ Find the Least Common Denominator (LCD) if necessary. ✓ Add whole numbers and fractions. ✓ Write your answer in lowest terms.
Example	**Add mixed numbers.** $1\frac{1}{2} + 2\frac{2}{3} =$ Rewriting our equation with parts separated, $1 + \frac{1}{2} + 2 + \frac{2}{3}$ Add whole numbers: $1 + 2 = 3$ Add fractions: $\frac{1}{2} + \frac{2}{3} = \frac{3}{6} + \frac{4}{6} = \frac{7}{6} = 1\frac{1}{6}$ Now, combine the whole and fraction parts: $3 + 1 + \frac{1}{6} = 4\frac{1}{6}$
Your Turn!	1) $1\frac{1}{12} + 2\frac{3}{4} = 3\frac{5}{6}$ 2) $3\frac{5}{8} + 1\frac{1}{4} = 4\frac{7}{8}$ 3) $1\frac{1}{10} + 2\frac{2}{5} = 3\frac{1}{2}$ 4) $2\frac{5}{6} + 2\frac{2}{9} = 5\frac{1}{18}$ 5) $2\frac{2}{7} + 1\frac{2}{21} = 3\frac{8}{21}$ 6) $1\frac{3}{8} + 3\frac{2}{3} = 5\frac{1}{24}$ 7) $3\frac{1}{5} + 1\frac{2}{8} = 4\frac{9}{20}$ 8) $3\frac{1}{2} + 2\frac{3}{7} = 5\frac{13}{14}$

Name: ....   **Date:** ....

Topic	**Subtracting Mixed Numbers**
Notes	Use the following steps for subtracting mixed numbers. ✓ Convert mixed numbers into improper fractions. $a\dfrac{c}{b} = \dfrac{ab+c}{b}$ ✓ Find equivalent fractions with the same denominator for unlike fractions (fractions with different denominators) ✓ Subtract the second fraction from the first one. ✓ Write your answer in lowest terms and convert it into a mixed number if the answer is an improper fraction.
Example	**Subtract.** $5\dfrac{1}{2} - 2\dfrac{2}{3} =$ Convert mixed numbers into fractions: $5\dfrac{1}{2} = \dfrac{5\times2+1}{5} = \dfrac{11}{2}$ and $2\dfrac{2}{3} = \dfrac{2\times3+2}{4} = \dfrac{8}{3}$, these two fractions are "unlike" fractions. (they have different denominators). Find equivalent fractions with the same denominator. Use this formula: $\dfrac{a}{b} - \dfrac{c}{d} = \dfrac{ad\ bc}{bd}$ $\dfrac{11}{2} - \dfrac{8}{3} = \dfrac{(11)(3)-(2)(8)}{2\times3} = \dfrac{33-16}{6} = \dfrac{17}{6}$, the answer is an improper fraction, convert it into a mixed number. $\qquad \dfrac{17}{6} = 2\dfrac{5}{6}$
Your Turn!	1) $2\dfrac{2}{5} - 1\dfrac{1}{3} =$ 2) $3\dfrac{5}{8} - 2\dfrac{1}{3} =$ 3) $6\dfrac{1}{4} - 1\dfrac{2}{7} =$ 4) $8\dfrac{2}{3} - 1\dfrac{1}{4} =$ 5) $8\dfrac{3}{4} - 1\dfrac{3}{8} =$ 6) $2\dfrac{3}{8} - 1\dfrac{2}{3} =$ 7) $13\dfrac{2}{7} - 1\dfrac{2}{21} =$ 8) $5\dfrac{1}{2} - 2\dfrac{3}{7} =$

Name:	Date: ....

Topic	**Subtracting Mixed Numbers - Answers**
Notes	Use the following steps for subtracting mixed numbers. ✓ Convert mixed numbers into improper fractions. $a\frac{c}{b} = \frac{ab+c}{b}$ ✓ Find equivalent fractions with the same denominator for unlike fractions (fractions with different denominators) ✓ Subtract the second fraction from the first one. ✓ Write your answer in lowest terms and convert it into a mixed number if the answer is an improper fraction.
Example	***Subtract.*** $5\frac{1}{2} - 2\frac{2}{3} =$ Convert mixed numbers into fractions: $5\frac{1}{2} = \frac{5\times2+1}{5} = \frac{11}{2}$ and $2\frac{2}{3} = \frac{2\times3+2}{4} = \frac{8}{3}$, these two fractions are "unlike" fractions. (they have different denominators). Find equivalent fractions with the same denominator. Use this formula: $\frac{a}{b} - \frac{c}{d} = \frac{ad-bc}{bd}$ $\frac{11}{2} - \frac{8}{3} = \frac{(11)(3)-(2)(8)}{2\times3} = \frac{33-1}{6} = \frac{17}{6}$, the answer is an improper fraction, convert it into a mixed number. $\frac{17}{6} = 2\frac{5}{6}$

Your Turn!	1) $2\frac{2}{5} - 1\frac{1}{3} = 1\frac{1}{15}$	2) $3\frac{5}{8} - 2\frac{1}{3} = 1\frac{7}{24}$
	3) $6\frac{1}{4} - 1\frac{2}{7} = 4\frac{27}{28}$	4) $8\frac{2}{3} - 1\frac{1}{4} = 7\frac{5}{12}$
	5) $8\frac{3}{4} - 1\frac{3}{8} = 7\frac{3}{8}$	6) $2\frac{3}{8} - 1\frac{2}{3} = \frac{17}{24}$
	7) $13\frac{2}{7} - 1\frac{2}{21} = 12\frac{4}{21}$	8) $5\frac{1}{2} - 2\frac{3}{7} = 3\frac{1}{14}$

Name: .... 　　　**Date:** ....

Topic	**Multiplying Mixed Numbers**
Notes	✓ Convert the mixed numbers into fractions. $a\frac{c}{b} = a + \frac{c}{b} = \frac{ab+c}{b}$ ✓ Multiply fractions and simplify if necessary. $\frac{a}{b} \times \frac{c}{d} = \frac{a \times c}{b \times d}$ ✓ If the answer is an improper fraction (numerator is bigger than denominator), convert it into a mixed number.
Example	**Multiply** $2\frac{1}{4} \times 3\frac{1}{2}$ Convert mixed numbers into fractions: $2\frac{1}{4} = \frac{2 \times 4 + 1}{4} = \frac{9}{4}$ and $3\frac{1}{2} = \frac{3 \times 2 + 1}{2} = \frac{7}{2}$ Multiply two fractions: $\frac{9}{4} \times \frac{7}{2} = \frac{9 \times 7}{4 \times 2} = \frac{63}{8}$ The answer is an improper fraction. Convert it into a mixed number: $$\frac{63}{8} = 7\frac{7}{8}$$
Your Turn!	1) $5\frac{2}{3} \times 2\frac{2}{9} =$ 　　　　　 2) $4\frac{1}{6} \times 5\frac{3}{7} =$ 3) $3\frac{1}{3} \times 3\frac{3}{4} =$ 　　　　　 4) $2\frac{2}{9} \times 6\frac{1}{3} =$ 5) $2\frac{2}{7} \times 4\frac{3}{5} =$ 　　　　　 6) $1\frac{4}{7} \times 9\frac{1}{2} =$ 7) $4\frac{1}{8} \times 3\frac{2}{3} =$ 　　　　　 8) $6\frac{2}{3} \times 1\frac{1}{4} =$

Name:	Date: ....

Topic	**Multiplying Mixed Numbers - Answers**
Notes	✓ Convert the mixed numbers into fractions. $a\frac{c}{b} = a + \frac{c}{b} = \frac{ab+c}{b}$ ✓ Multiply fractions and simplify if necessary. $\frac{a}{b} \times \frac{c}{d} = \frac{a \times c}{b \times d}$ ✓ If the answer is an improper fraction (numerator is bigger than denominator), convert it into a mixed number.
Example	***Multiply*** $2\frac{1}{4} \times 3\frac{1}{2}$ Convert mixed numbers into fractions: $2\frac{1}{4} = \frac{2 \times 4 + 1}{4} = \frac{9}{4}$ and $3\frac{1}{2} = \frac{3 \times 2 + 1}{2} = \frac{7}{2}$ Multiply two fractions: $\frac{9}{4} \times \frac{7}{2} = \frac{9 \times 7}{4 \times 2} = \frac{63}{8}$ The answer is an improper fraction. Convert it into a mixed number: $$\frac{63}{8} = 7\frac{7}{8}$$
Your Turn!	1) $5\frac{2}{3} \times 2\frac{2}{9} = 12\frac{16}{27}$ 2) $4\frac{1}{6} \times 5\frac{3}{7} = 22\frac{13}{21}$ 3) $3\frac{1}{3} \times 3\frac{3}{4} = 12\frac{1}{2}$ 4) $2\frac{2}{9} \times 6\frac{1}{3} = 14\frac{2}{27}$ 5) $2\frac{2}{7} \times 4\frac{3}{5} = 10\frac{18}{35}$ 6) $1\frac{4}{7} \times 9\frac{1}{2} = 14\frac{13}{14}$ 7) $4\frac{1}{8} \times 3\frac{2}{3} = 15\frac{1}{8}$ 8) $6\frac{2}{3} \times 1\frac{1}{4} = 8\frac{1}{3}$

Name:	Date: ....

Topic	**Dividing Mixed Numbers**	
Notes	✓ Convert the mixed numbers into improper fractions. $$a\frac{c}{b} = a + \frac{c}{b} = \frac{ab+c}{b}$$ ✓ Divide fractions and simplify if necessary.	
Example	*Solve.* $2\frac{1}{3} \div 1\frac{1}{4} =$ Converting mixed numbers to fractions: $2\frac{1}{3} \div 1\frac{1}{4} = \frac{7}{3} \div \frac{5}{4}$ Keep, Change, Flip: $\frac{7}{3} \div \frac{5}{4} = \frac{7}{3} \times \frac{4}{5} = \frac{7 \times 4}{3 \times 5} = \frac{28}{15} = 1\frac{13}{15}$	
Your Turn!	1) $3\frac{2}{7} \div 2\frac{1}{4} =$	2) $4\frac{2}{9} \div 1\frac{5}{6} =$
	3) $4\frac{2}{3} \div 3\frac{2}{5} =$	4) $5\frac{4}{5} \div 4\frac{3}{4} =$
	5) $1\frac{8}{9} \div 2\frac{3}{7} =$	6) $3\frac{3}{8} \div 2\frac{2}{5} =$
	7) $4\frac{1}{5} \div 3\frac{1}{9} =$	8) $4\frac{2}{3} \div 1\frac{8}{9} =$
	9) $5\frac{2}{3} \div 3\frac{3}{7} =$	10) $7\frac{1}{2} \div 5\frac{1}{3} =$

| Name: .... | Date: .... |

Topic	**Dividing Mixed Numbers- Answers**
Notes	✓ Convert the mixed numbers into improper fractions. $$a\frac{c}{b} = a + \frac{c}{b} = \frac{ab + c}{b}$$ ✓ Divide fractions and simplify if necessary.
Example	*Solve.* $2\frac{1}{3} \div 1\frac{1}{4} =$ Converting mixed numbers to fractions: $2\frac{1}{3} \div 1\frac{1}{4} = \frac{7}{3} \div \frac{5}{4}$ Keep, Change, Flip: $\frac{7}{3} \div \frac{5}{4} = \frac{7}{3} \times \frac{4}{5} = \frac{7 \times 4}{3 \times 5} = \frac{28}{15} = 1\frac{13}{15}$

Your Turn!	1) $3\frac{2}{7} \div 2\frac{1}{4} = 1\frac{29}{63}$	2) $4\frac{2}{9} \div 1\frac{5}{6} = 2\frac{10}{33}$
	3) $4\frac{2}{3} \div 3\frac{2}{5} = 1\frac{19}{51}$	4) $5\frac{4}{5} \div 4\frac{3}{4} = 1\frac{21}{95}$
	5) $1\frac{8}{9} \div 2\frac{3}{7} = \frac{7}{9}$	6) $3\frac{3}{8} \div 2\frac{2}{5} = 1\frac{13}{32}$
	7) $4\frac{1}{5} \div 3\frac{1}{9} = 1\frac{7}{20}$	8) $4\frac{2}{3} \div 1\frac{8}{9} = 2\frac{8}{17}$
	9) $5\frac{2}{3} \div 3\frac{3}{7} = 1\frac{47}{72}$	10) $7\frac{1}{2} \div 5\frac{1}{3} = 1\frac{13}{32}$

Name: ....   **Date:** ....

Topic	Comparing Decimals
Notes	Decimals: is a fraction written in a special form. For example, instead of writing $\frac{1}{2}$ you can write **0.5**. For comparing decimals: ✓ Compare each digit of two decimals in the same place value. ✓ Start from left. Compare hundreds, tens, ones, tenth, hundredth, etc. ✓ To compare numbers, use these symbols: - Equal to =, Less than <, Greater than > Greater than or equal ≥, Less than or equal ≤
Examples	***Compare 0.40 and 0.04.*** 0.40 *is greater than* 0.04, because the tenth place of 0.40 is 4, but the tenth place of 0.04 is zero. Then: $0.40 > 0.04$ ***Compare 0.0912 and 0.912.*** 0.912 *is greater than* 0.0912, because the tenth place of 0.912 is 9, but the tenth place of 0.0912 is zero. Then: $0.0912 < 0.912$

Your Turn!	1) 0.91 ☐ 0.95	2) 1.79 ☐ 1.80
	3) 19.1 ☐ 19.09	4) 2.45 ☐ 2.089
	5) 1.258 ☐ 12.58	6) 0.89 ☐ 0.890
	7) 3.871 ☐ 2.998	8) 0.567 ☐ 0.756

Name:	Date: ....

Topic	**Comparing Decimals - Answers**
Notes	Decimals: is a fraction written in a special form. For example, instead of writing $\frac{1}{2}$ you can write **0.5**. For comparing decimals: ✓ Compare each digit of two decimals in the same place value. ✓ Start from left. Compare hundreds, tens, ones, tenth, hundredth, etc. ✓ To compare numbers, use these symbols: - Equal to =, Less than <, Greater than > Greater than or equal ≥, Less than or equal ≤
Examples	**Compare 0.40 and 0.04.** 0.40 *is greater than* 0.04, because the tenth place of 0.40 is 4, but the tenth place of 0.04 is zero. Then: $0.40 > 0.04$ **Compare 0.0912 and 0.912.** 0.912 *is greater than* 0.0912, because the tenth place of 0.912 is 9, but the tenth place of 0.0912 is zero. Then: $0.0912 < 0.912$

Your Turn!	1) $0.91 < 0.95$	2) $1.78 < 1.80$
	3) $19.1 > 19.09$	4) $2.45 > 2.089$
	5) $1.258 < 12.58$	6) $0.89 = 0.890$
	7) $3.387 > 2.998$	8) $0.567 < 0.756$

| Name: .... | Date: .... |

Topic	**Rounding Decimals**
Notes	✓ We can round decimals to a certain accuracy or number of decimal places. ✓ Let's review place values: For example: **35.4817** 3: tens 5: ones 4: tenths 8: hundredths 1: thousandths 7: tens thousandths ✓ To round a decimal, find the place value you'll round to. ✓ Find the digit to the right of the place value you're rounding to. If it is 5 or bigger, add 1 to the place value you're rounding to and remove all digits on its right side. If the digit to the right of the place value is less than 5, keep the place value and remove all digits on the right.
Example	**Round 12.8365 to the hundredth place value.** First look at the next place value to the right, (thousandths). It's 6 and it is greater than 5. Thus add 1 to the digit in the hundredth place. It is 3. → $3 + 1 = 4$, then, the answer is 12.84
Your Turn!	**Round each number to the underlined place value.** 1) 32.5$\underline{4}$8 = 2) 2.3$\underline{2}$6 = 3) 55.$\underline{4}$23 = 4) 2$\underline{5}$.62 = 5) 11.$\underline{2}$65 = 6) 33.5$\underline{0}$5 = 7) 3.5$\underline{8}$9 = 8) 8.0$\underline{1}$9 =

Name: ....

Date: ....

Topic	**Rounding Decimals – Answers**
Notes	✓ We can round decimals to a certain accuracy or number of decimal places. ✓ Let's review place values: For example: **35.4817** 3: tens 5: ones 4: tenths 8: hundredths 1: thousandths 7: tens thousandths ✓ To round a decimal, find the place value you'll round to. ✓ Find the digit to the right of the place value you're rounding to. If it is 5 or bigger, add 1 to the place value you're rounding to and remove all digits on its right side. If the digit to the right of the place value is less than 5, keep the place value and remove all digits on the right.
Example	***Round 12.8365 to the hundredth place value.*** First look at the next place value to the right, (thousandths). It's 6 and it is greater than 5. Thus add 1 to the digit in the hundredth place. It is 3. → $3 + 1 = 4$, then, the answer is 12.84

Round each number to the underlined place value.

1) $32.5\underline{4}8 = 32.55$	2) $2.3\underline{2}6 = 2.33$
3) $55.\underline{4}23 = 55.4$	4) $2\underline{5}.62 = 26$
5) $11.\underline{2}65 = 11.3$	6) $33.5\underline{0}5 = 33.51$
7) $3.5\underline{8}9 = 3.59$	8) $8.0\underline{1}9 = 8.02$

Name: .... **Date:** ....

Topic	Adding and Subtracting Decimals
Notes	✓ Line up the numbers. ✓ Add zeros to have same number of digits for both numbers if necessary. ✓ Add or subtract using column addition or subtraction.
Examples	***Add***. $2.6 + 5.33 =$ First line up the numbers: $\begin{array}{r} 2.6 \\ + 5.33 \\ \hline \end{array}$ →Add zeros to have same number of digits for both numbers. $\begin{array}{r} 2.60 \\ + 5.33 \\ \hline \end{array}$ → Start with the hundredths place. $0 + 3 = 2$, $\begin{array}{r} 2.60 \\ + 5.33 \\ \hline 3 \end{array}$ → Continue with tenths place. $6 + 3 = 9$, $\begin{array}{r} 2.60 \\ + 5.33 \\ \hline .93 \end{array}$ → Add the ones place. $2 + 5 = 7$, $\begin{array}{r} 2.60 \\ + 5.33 \\ \hline 7.93 \end{array}$ ***Subtract***. $4.79 - 3.13 =$ $\begin{array}{r} 4.79 \\ - 3.13 \\ \hline \end{array}$ Start with the hundredths place. $9 - 3 = 6$, $\begin{array}{r} 4.79 \\ - 3.13 \\ \hline 6 \end{array}$, continue with tenths place. $7 - 1 = 6$, $\begin{array}{r} 4.79 \\ - 3.13 \\ \hline .66 \end{array}$, subtract the ones place. $4 - 3 = 1$, $\begin{array}{r} 4.79 \\ - 3.13 \\ \hline 1.66 \end{array}$
Your Turn!	1) $48.13 + 20.15 =$ 2) $78.14 - 65.19 =$ 3) $38.19 + 24.18 =$ 4) $57.26 - 43.54 =$ 5) $27.89 + 46.13 =$ 6) $49.65 - 32.78 =$

Name:	Date: ....

Topic	**Adding and Subtracting Decimals - Answers**
Notes	✓ Line up the numbers. ✓ Add zeros to have same number of digits for both numbers if necessary. ✓ Add or subtract using column addition or subtraction.
Examples	**Add.** $2.6 + 5.33 =$ First line up the numbers: $\begin{array}{r} 2.6 \\ +5.33 \\ \hline \end{array}$ →Add zeros to have same number of digits for both numbers. $\begin{array}{r} 2.60 \\ +5.33 \\ \hline \end{array}$ → Start with the hundredths place. $0 + 3 = 2$, $\begin{array}{r} 2.60 \\ +5.33 \\ \hline 3 \end{array}$ → Continue with tenths place. $6 + 3 = 9$, $\begin{array}{r} 2.60 \\ +5.33 \\ \hline .93 \end{array}$ → Add the ones place. $2 + 5 = 7$, $\begin{array}{r} 2.60 \\ +5.33 \\ \hline 7.93 \end{array}$ **Subtract.** $4.79 - 3.13 =$ $\begin{array}{r} 4.79 \\ -3.13 \\ \hline \end{array}$ Start with the hundredths place. $9 - 3 = 6$, $\begin{array}{r} 4.79 \\ -3.13 \\ \hline 6 \end{array}$, continue with tenths place. $7 - 1 = 6$, $\begin{array}{r} 4.79 \\ -3.13 \\ \hline .66 \end{array}$, subtract the ones place. $4 - 3 = 1$, $\begin{array}{r} 4.79 \\ -3.13 \\ \hline 1.66 \end{array}$
Your Turn!	1) $48.13 + 20.15 = 68.28$ 2) $78.14 - 65.19 = 12.95$ 3) $38.19 + 24.18 = 62.37$ 4) $57.26 - 43.54 = 13.72$ 5) $27.89 + 46.13 = 74.02$ 6) $49.65 - 32.78 = 16.87$

Name: .... **Date:** ....

Topic	**Multiplying and Dividing Decimals**
Notes	For Multiplication: ✓ Ignore the decimal point and set up and multiply the numbers as you do with whole numbers. ✓ Count the total number of decimal places in both factors. ✓ Place the decimal point in the product. For Division: ✓ If the divisor is not a whole number, move decimal point to right to make it a whole number. Do the same for dividend. ✓ Divide similar to whole numbers.
Examples	***Find the product.*** $1.2 \times 2.3 =$ Set up and multiply the numbers as you do with whole numbers. Line up the numbers: $\begin{array}{r} 12 \\ \times 23 \end{array} \rightarrow$ Multiply: $\frac{\begin{array}{r} 12 \\ \times 23 \end{array}}{276} \rightarrow$ Count the total number of decimal places in both of the factors. There are two decimal digits. Then: $1.2 \times 2.3 = 2.76$ ***Find the quotient.*** $5.6 \div 0.8 =$ The divisor is not a whole number. Multiply it by 10 to get 8. $\rightarrow 0.8 \times 10 = 8$ Do the same for the dividend to get 56 $\rightarrow 5.6 \times 10 = 56$ Now, divide: $56 \div 8 = 7$. The answer is 7.
Your Turn!	1) $1.13 \times 0.7 =$ 2) $48.8 \div 8 =$ 3) $0.9 \times 0.68 =$ 4) $66.8 \div 0.2 =$ 5) $0.18 \times 0.5 =$ 6) $37.2 \div 100 =$

Name:	**Date:** ....

Topic	**Multiplying and Dividing Decimals - Answers**
Notes	For Multiplication: ✓ Ignore the decimal point and set up and multiply the numbers as you do with whole numbers. ✓ Count the total number of decimal places in both factors. ✓ Place the decimal point in the product. For Division: ✓ If the divisor is not a whole number, move decimal point to right to make it a whole number. Do the same for dividend. ✓ Divide similar to whole numbers.
Examples	***Find the product.*** $1.2 \times 2.3 =$ Set up and multiply the numbers as you do with whole numbers. Line up the numbers: $\begin{matrix}12\\ \times 23\\ \hline\end{matrix} \rightarrow$ Multiply: $\begin{matrix}12\\ \times 23\\ \hline 276\end{matrix} \rightarrow$ Count the total number of decimal places in both of the factors. There are two decimal digits. Then: $1.2 \times 2.3 = 2.76$ ***Find the quotient.*** $5.6 \div 0.8 =$ The divisor is not a whole number. Multiply it by 10 to get 8. $\rightarrow 0.8 \times 10 = 8$ Do the same for the dividend to get 56 $\rightarrow 5.6 \times 10 = 56$ Now, divide: $56 \div 8 = 7$. The answer is 7.
Your Turn!	1) $1.13 \times 0.7 = 0.791$ 2) $48.8 \div 8 = 6.1$ 3) $0.9 \times 0.68 = 0.612$ 4) $66.8 \div 0.2 = 334$ 5) $0.18 \times 0.5 = 0.09$ 6) $37.2 \div 100 = 0.372$

Name:	Date: ....

Topic	**Adding and Subtracting Integers**
Notes	✓ Integers include: zero, counting numbers, and the negative of the counting numbers. $\{... , -3, -2, -1, 0, 1, 2, 3, ...\}$ ✓ Add a positive integer by moving to the right on the number line. ✓ Add a negative integer by moving to the left on the number line. Subtract an integer by adding its opposite.
Examples	***Solve.*** $(4) - (-8) =$ Keep the first number and convert the sign of the second number to its opposite. (change subtraction into addition. Then: $(4) + 8 = 12$ ***Solve.*** $42 + (12 - 26) =$ First subtract the numbers in brackets, $12 - 26 = -14$ Then: $42 + (-14) = \rightarrow$ change addition into subtraction: $42 - 14 = 28$
Your Turn!	1) $-(15) + 12 =$ 2) $(-2) + (-10) + 18 =$ 3) $(-13) + 7 =$ 4) $3 - (-7) + 14 =$ 5) $(-7) + (-8) =$ 6) $16 - (-4 + 8) =$ 7) $4 + (-15) + 2 =$ 8) $-(22) - (-4) + 8 =$

Name:	Date: ....

Topic	**Adding and Subtracting Integers - Answers**
Notes	✓ Integers include: zero, counting numbers, and the negative of the counting numbers. $\{... , -3, -2, -1, 0, 1, 2, 3, ...\}$ ✓ Add a positive integer by moving to the right on the number line. ✓ Add a negative integer by moving to the left on the number line. Subtract an integer by adding its opposite.
Examples	*Solve*. $(4) - (-8) =$ Keep the first number and convert the sign of the second number to its opposite. (change subtraction into addition. Then: $(4) + 8 = 12$ *Solve.* $42 + (12 - 26) =$ First subtract the numbers in brackets, $12 - 26 = -14$ Then: $42 + (-14) = \rightarrow$ change addition into subtraction: $42 - 14 = 28$

Your Turn!	1) $-(15) + 12 = -3$	2) $(-2) + (-10) + 18 = 6$
	3) $(-13) + 7 = -6$	4) $3 - (-7) + 14 = 24$
	5) $(-7) + (-8) = -15$	6) $16 - (-4 + 8) = 12$
	7) $4 + (-15) + 2 = -9$	8) $(-22) - (-4) + 8 = -10$

Name: .... **Date:** ....

Topic	**Multiplying and Dividing Integers**
Notes	Use following rules for multiplying and dividing integers: ✓ (negative) × (negative) = positive ✓ (negative) ÷ (negative) = positive ✓ (negative) × (positive) = negative ✓ (negative) ÷ (positive) = negative ✓ (positive) × (positive) = positive ✓ (positive) ÷ (negative) = negative
Examples	**Solve**. $2 \times (14 - 17) =$ First subtract the numbers in brackets, $14 - 17 = -3 \rightarrow (2) \times (-3) =$ Now use this rule: (positive) × (negative) = negative $(2) \times (-3) = -6$ **Solve**. $(-7) + (-36 \div 4) =$ First divide -36 by 4, the numbers in brackets, using this rule: (negative) ÷ (positive) = negative Then: $-36 \div 4 = -9$. Now, add -7 and -9: $(-7) + (-9) = -7 - 9 = -16$

Your Turn!		
	1) $(-7) \times 6 =$	2) $(-63) \div (-7) =$
	3) $(-11) \times (-3) =$	4) $81 \div (-9) =$
	5) $(15 - 12) \times (-7) =$	6) $(-12) \div (3) =$
	7) $4 \times (-9) =$	8) $(8) \div (-2) =$

Name:	Date: ....

Topic	**Multiplying and Dividing Integers - Answers**
Notes	Use following rules for multiplying and dividing integers: ✓ (negative) × (negative) = positive ✓ (negative) ÷ (negative) = positive ✓ (negative) × (positive) = negative ✓ (negative) ÷ (positive) = negative ✓ (positive) × (positive) = positive ✓ (positive) ÷ (negative) = negative
Examples	**Solve.** $2 \times (14 - 17) =$ First subtract the numbers in brackets, $14 - 17 = -3 \rightarrow (2) \times (-3) =$ Now use this rule: (positive) × (negative) = negative $(2) \times (-3) = -6$ **Solve.** $(-7) + (-36 \div 4) =$ First divide -36 by 4, the numbers in brackets, using this rule: (negative) ÷ (positive) = negative Then: $-36 \div 4 = -9$. Now, add -7 and -9: $(-7) + (-9) = -7 - 9 = -16$

Your Turn!		
	1) $(-7) \times 6 = -42$	2) $(-63) \div (-7) = 9$
	3) $(-11) \times (-3) = 33$	4) $81 \div (-9) = -9$
	5) $(15 - 12) \times (-7) = -21$	6) $(-12) \div (3) = -4$
	7) $4 \times (-9) = -36$	8) $(8) \div (-2) = -4$

| Name: .... | Date: .... |

Topic	**Order of Operation**	
Notes	When there is more than one math operation, use PEMDAS: (to memorize this rule, remember the phrase "Please Excuse My Dear Aunt Sally") ✓ Parentheses ✓ Exponents ✓ Multiplication and Division (from left to right) ✓ Addition and Subtraction (from left to right)	
Examples	*Calculate.* $(18 - 26) \div (2^4 \div 4) =$ First simplify inside parentheses: $(-8) \div (16 \div 4) = (-8) \div (4)$ Then: $(-8) \div (4) = -2$ *Solve.* $(-5 \times 7) - (18 - 3^2) =$ First calculate within parentheses: $(-5 \times 7) - (18 - 3^2) = (-35) - (18 - 9)$ Then: $(-35) - (18 - 9) = -35 - 9 = -44$	
Your Turn!	1) $(11 \times 4) \div (5 + 6) =$	2) $(30 \div 5) + (17 - 8) =$
	3) $(-9) + (5 \times 6) + 14 =$	4) $(-10 \times 5) \div (2^2 + 1) =$
	5) $[-16(32 \div 2^3)] \div 8 =$	6) $(-7) + (72 \div 3^2) + 12 =$
	7) $[16(32 \div 2^3)] - 4^2 =$	8) $4^3 + (-5 \times 2^5) + 5 =$

Name:	Date: ....

Topic	Order of Operation - Answers
Notes	When there is more than one math operation, use PEMDAS: (to memorize this rule, remember the phrase "Please Excuse My Dear Aunt Sally") ✓ Parentheses ✓ Exponents ✓ Multiplication and Division (from left to right) ✓ Addition and Subtraction (from left to right)
Examples	***Calculate.*** $(18 - 26) \div (2^4 \div 4) =$ First simplify inside parentheses: $(-8) \div (16 \div 4) = (-8) \div (4)$ Then: $(-8) \div (4) = -2$ ***Solve.*** $(-5 \times 7) - (18 - 3^2) =$ First calculate within parentheses: $(-5 \times 7) - (18 - 3^2) = (-35) - (18 - 9)$ Then: $(-35) - (18 - 9) = -35 - 9 = -44$

Your Turn!	1) $(11 \times 4) \div (5 + 6) = 4$	2) $(30 \div 5) + (17 - 8) = 15$
	3) $(-9) + (5 \times 6) + 14 =$ 35	4) $(-10 \times 5) \div (2^2 + 1) = -10$
	5) $[-16(32 \div 2^3)] \div 8 =$ -8	6) $(-7) + (72 \div 3^2) + 12 = 13$
	7) $[16(32 \div 2^3)] - 4^2 =$ 48	8) $4^3 + (-5 \times 2^5) + 5 = -91$

Name:	Date: ....

Topic	**Integers and Absolute Value**
Notes	✓ The absolute value of a number is its distance from zero, in either direction, on the number line. For example, the distance of 9 and -9 from zero on number line is 9. ✓ Absolute value is symbolized by vertical bars, as in $|x|$.
Example	*Calculate.* $\|8-5\| \times \|12-16\| =$ First calculate $\|8-5\|$, $\rightarrow \|8-5\| = \|3\|$, the absolute value of 3 is 3, $\|3\| = 3$ $8 \times \|12-16\| =$ Now calculate $\|12-16\|$, $\rightarrow \|12-16\| = \|-4\|$, the absolute value of -4 is 4, $\|-4\| = 4$. Then: $3 \times 4 = 12$
Your Turn!	1) $11 - \|4 - 13\| =$ 2) $14 - \|12 - 19\| - \|9\| =$ 3) $\|21\| - \dfrac{\|-25\|}{5} =$ 4) $\|30\| + \dfrac{\|-49\|}{7} =$ 5) $\dfrac{\|7 \times -8\|}{4} \times \dfrac{\|-12\|}{2} =$ 6) $\dfrac{\|10 \times -6\|}{5} \times \|-9\| =$ 7) $\dfrac{\|-20\|}{5} \times \dfrac{\|-36\|}{6} =$ 8) $\|-30 + 6\| \times \dfrac{\|-9 \times 4\|}{12} =$

| Name: .... | Date: .... |

Topic	Integers and Absolute Value - Answers	
Notes	✓ The absolute value of a number is its distance from zero, in either direction, on the number line. For example, the distance of 9 and -9 from zero on number line is 9. ✓ Absolute value is symbolized by vertical bars, as in $\lvert x \rvert$.	
Example	*Calculate.* $\lvert 8-5 \rvert \times \lvert 12-16 \rvert =$ First calculate $\lvert 8-5 \rvert$, $\rightarrow \lvert 8-5 \rvert = \lvert 3 \rvert$, the absolute value of 3 is 3, $\lvert 3 \rvert = 3$ $8 \times \lvert 12-16 \rvert =$ Now calculate $\lvert 12-16 \rvert$, $\rightarrow \lvert 12-16 \rvert = \lvert -4 \rvert$, the absolute value of -4 is 4, $\lvert -4 \rvert = 4$. Then: $3 \times 4 = 12$	
Your Turn!	1) $11 - \lvert 4-13 \rvert = 2$	2) $14 - \lvert 12-19 \rvert - \lvert 9 \rvert = -2$
	3) $\lvert 21 \rvert - \dfrac{\lvert -25 \rvert}{5} = 16$	4) $\lvert 30 \rvert + \dfrac{\lvert -49 \rvert}{7} = 37$
	5) $\dfrac{\lvert 7 \times -8 \rvert}{4} \times \dfrac{\lvert -12 \rvert}{2} = 84$	6) $\dfrac{\lvert 10 \times -6 \rvert}{5} \times \lvert -9 \rvert = 108$
	7) $\dfrac{\lvert -20 \rvert}{5} \times \dfrac{\lvert -36 \rvert}{6} = 24$	8) $\lvert -30 + 6 \rvert \times \dfrac{\lvert -9 \times 4 \rvert}{12} = 72$

Name:	Date: ....

Topic	**Simplifying Ratios**
Notes	✓ Ratios are used to make comparisons between two numbers. ✓ Ratios can be written as a fraction, using the word "to", or with a colon. ✓ You can calculate equivalent ratios by multiplying or dividing both sides of the ratio by the same number.
Examples	***Simplify.*** $18:63 =$ Both numbers 18 and 63 are divisible by $9 \Rightarrow 18 \div 9 = 2, 63 \div 9 = 7,$ Then: $18:63 = 2:7$ ***Simplify.*** $\dfrac{25}{45} =$ Both numbers 25 and 45 are divisible by 5, $\Rightarrow 25 \div 5 = 5, 45 \div 5 = 9,$ Then: $\dfrac{25}{45} = \dfrac{5}{9}$
Your Turn!	1) $\dfrac{4}{32} = -$ 2) $\dfrac{25}{80} = -$ 3) $\dfrac{15}{35} = -$ 4) $\dfrac{42}{54} = -$ 5) $\dfrac{12}{36} = -$ 6) $\dfrac{30}{80} = -$ 7) $\dfrac{18}{24} = -$ 8) $\dfrac{60}{108} = -$

| Name: .... | Date: .... |

Topic	**Simplifying Ratios - Answers**	
Notes	✓ Ratios are used to make comparisons between two numbers. ✓ Ratios can be written as a fraction, using the word "to", or with a colon. ✓ You can calculate equivalent ratios by multiplying or dividing both sides of the ratio by the same number.	
Examples	***Simplify.*** $18 : 63 =$ Both numbers 18 and 63 are divisible by $9 \Rightarrow 18 \div 9 = 2, 63 \div 9 = 7$, Then: $18 : 63 = 2 : 7$ ***Simplify.*** $\frac{25}{45} =$ Both numbers 25 and 45 are divisible by 5, $\Rightarrow 25 \div 5 = 5, 45 \div 5 = 9$, Then: $\frac{25}{45} = \frac{5}{9}$	
Your Turn!	1) $\frac{4}{32} = \frac{1}{8}$	2) $\frac{25}{80} = \frac{5}{16}$
	3) $\frac{15}{35} = \frac{3}{7}$	4) $\frac{42}{54} = \frac{7}{9}$
	5) $\frac{12}{36} = \frac{1}{3}$	6) $\frac{30}{80} = \frac{3}{8}$ 7)
	8) $\frac{18}{24} = \frac{3}{4}$	9) $\frac{60}{108} = \frac{5}{9}$

Name:	Date: ....

Topic	**Proportional Ratios**
Notes	✓ Two ratios are proportional if they represent the same relationship. ✓ A proportion means that two ratios are equal. It can be written in two ways: $$\frac{a}{b} = \frac{c}{d} \qquad a:b = c:d$$
Example	***Solve this proportion for*** x. $\frac{5}{8} = \frac{35}{x}$ Use cross multiplication: $\frac{5}{8} = \frac{35}{x} \Rightarrow 5 \times x = 8 \times 35 \Rightarrow 5x = 280$ Divide to find x: $x = \frac{280}{5} \Rightarrow x = 56$
Your Turn!	1) $\frac{1}{9} = \frac{8}{x} \Rightarrow x =$ ____ 2) $\frac{5}{8} = \frac{25}{x} \Rightarrow x =$ ____ 3) $\frac{3}{11} = \frac{6}{x} \Rightarrow x =$ ____ 4) $\frac{12}{20} = \frac{x}{200} \Rightarrow x =$ ____ 5) $\frac{9}{12} = \frac{27}{x} \Rightarrow x =$ ____ 6) $\frac{14}{16} = \frac{x}{80} \Rightarrow x =$ ____ 7) $\frac{7}{15} = \frac{49}{x} \Rightarrow x =$ ____ 8) $\frac{8}{19} = \frac{32}{x} \Rightarrow x =$ ____

| Name: .... | Date: .... |

Topic	**Proportional Ratios - Answers**
Notes	✓ Two ratios are proportional if they represent the same relationship. ✓ A proportion means that two ratios are equal. It can be written in two ways: $$\frac{a}{b} = \frac{c}{d} \qquad a : b = c : d$$
Example	***Solve this proportion for*** x. $\frac{5}{8} = \frac{35}{x}$ Use cross multiplication: $\frac{5}{8} = \frac{35}{x} \Rightarrow 5 \times x = 8 \times 35 \Rightarrow 5x = 280$ Divide to find x: $\quad x = \frac{280}{5} \Rightarrow x = 56$

Your Turn!		
	1) $\frac{1}{9} = \frac{8}{x} \Rightarrow x = 72$	2) $\frac{5}{8} = \frac{25}{x} \Rightarrow x = 40$
	3) $\frac{3}{11} = \frac{6}{x} \Rightarrow x = 22$	4) $\frac{12}{20} = \frac{x}{200} \Rightarrow x = 120$
	5) $\frac{9}{12} = \frac{27}{x} \Rightarrow x = 36$	6) $\frac{14}{16} = \frac{x}{80} \Rightarrow x = 70$
	7) $\frac{7}{15} = \frac{49}{x} \Rightarrow x = 105$	8) $\frac{8}{19} = \frac{32}{x} \Rightarrow x = 76$

Name: ....

Date: ....

Topic	Create Proportion
Notes	✓ To create a proportion, simply find (or create) two equal fractions. ✓ Use cross products to solve proportions or to test whether two ratios are equal and form a proportion. $\frac{a}{b} = \frac{c}{d} \Rightarrow a \times d = c \times b$
Example	*State if this pair of ratios form a proportion.* $\frac{2}{3}$ *and* $\frac{12}{30}$ Use cross multiplication: $\frac{2}{3} = \frac{12}{30} \rightarrow 2 \times 30 = 12 \times 3 \rightarrow 60 = 36$, which is not correct. Therefore, this pair of ratios doesn't form a proportion.

Your Turn!

State if each pair of ratios form a proportion.

1) $\frac{4}{8}$ *and* $\frac{24}{48}$

2) $\frac{5}{15}$ *and* $\frac{10}{20}$

3) $\frac{3}{11}$ *and* $\frac{9}{33}$

4) $\frac{7}{10}$ *and* $\frac{14}{20}$

5) $\frac{7}{9}$ *and* $\frac{48}{81}$

6) $\frac{6}{8}$ *and* $\frac{12}{14}$

7) $\frac{2}{10}$ *and* $\frac{6}{30}$

8) $\frac{9}{12}$ *and* $\frac{18}{24}$

9) Solve.

Five pencils costs $0.65. How many pencils can you buy for $2.60? _____

| Name: .... | Date: .... |

Topic	Create Proportion
Notes	✓ To create a proportion, simply find (or create) two equal fractions. ✓ Use cross products to solve proportions or to test whether two ratios are equal and form a proportion. $\frac{a}{b} = \frac{c}{d} \Rightarrow a \times d = c \times b$
Example	***State if this pair of ratios form a proportion.*** $\frac{2}{3}$ *and* $\frac{12}{30}$ Use cross multiplication: $\frac{2}{3} = \frac{12}{30} \rightarrow 2 \times 30 = 12 \times 3 \rightarrow 60 = 36$, which is not correct. Therefore, this pair of ratios doesn't form a proportion.

	State if each pair of ratios form a proportion.	
Your Turn!	1) $\frac{4}{8}$ *and* $\frac{24}{48}$, *Yes*	2) $\frac{5}{15}$ *and* $\frac{10}{20}$, *No*
	3) $\frac{3}{11}$ *and* $\frac{9}{33}$, *Yes*	4) $\frac{7}{10}$ *and* $\frac{14}{20}$, *Yes*
	5) $\frac{7}{9}$ *and* $\frac{48}{81}$, *No*	6) $\frac{6}{8}$ *and* $\frac{12}{14}$, *No*
	7) $\frac{2}{10}$ *and* $\frac{6}{30}$, *Yes*	8) $\frac{9}{12}$ *and* $\frac{18}{24}$, *Yes*
	9) Solve. Five pencils costs $0.65. How many pencils can you buy for $2.60? **20 pencils**	

Name:	Date: ....

Topic	**Similarity and Ratios**
Notes	✓ Two figures are similar if they have the same shape. ✓ Two or more figures are similar if the corresponding angles are equal, and the corresponding sides are in proportion.
Example	*Following triangles are similar. What is the value of unknown side?* **Solution:** Find the corresponding sides and write a proportion: $\frac{4}{12} = \frac{x}{9}$. Now, use cross product to solve for x: $\frac{4}{12} = \frac{x}{9} \rightarrow 4 \times 9 = 12 \times x \rightarrow 36 = 12x$. Divide both sides by 12. Then: $5x = 40 \rightarrow \frac{36}{12} = \frac{12x}{12} \rightarrow x = 3$. The missing side is 3.
Your Turn!	1) 2) 3) 4) 5) 6)

Name:	Date: ....

Topic	**Similarity and Ratios - Answers**
Notes	✓ Two figures are similar if they have the same shape. ✓ Two or more figures are similar if the corresponding angles are equal, and the corresponding sides are in proportion.
Example	*Following triangles are similar. What is the value of unknown side?* **Solution:** Find the corresponding sides and write a proportion: $\frac{4}{12} = \frac{x}{9}$. Now, use cross product to solve for x: $\frac{4}{12} = \frac{x}{9} \rightarrow 4 \times 9 = 12 \times x \rightarrow 36 = 12x$. Divide both sides by 12. Then: $5x = 40 \rightarrow \frac{36}{12} = \frac{12}{12} \rightarrow x = 3$. The missing side is 3.
Your Turn!	1) 24 2) 11 3) 4 4) 8 5) 10 6) 9

Name:	Date: ....

Topic	**Percent Problems**	
Notes	✓ In each percent problem, we are looking for the base, or part or the percent. ✓ Use the following equations to find each missing section. ○ Base = Part ÷ Percent ○ Part = Percent × Base ○ Percent = Part ÷ Base	
Examples	**18 *is what percent of* 30?** In this problem, we are looking for the percent. Use the following equation: $Percent = Part \div Base \rightarrow Percent = 18 \div 30 = 0.6 = 60\%$ **40 *is* 20% *of what number?*** Use the following formula: $Base = Part \div Percent \rightarrow Base = 40 \div 0.20 = 200$ 40 is 20% of 200.	
Your Turn!	1) What is 25 percent of 800?	2) 26 is what percent of 200?
	3) 60 is 5 percent of what number?	4) 48 is what percent of 300?
	5) 84 is 28 percent of what number?	6) 63 is what percent of 700?
	7) 96 is 24 percent of what number?	8) 40 is what percent of 800?

Name:	Date: ....

Topic	**Percent Problems – Answers**
Notes	✓ In each percent problem, we are looking for the base, or part or the percent. ✓ Use the following equations to find each missing section. 　○ Base = Part ÷ Percent 　○ Part = Percent × Base 　○ Percent = Part ÷ Base
Examples	**18 *is what percent of* 30?** In this problem, we are looking for the percent. Use the following equation: $Percent = Part \div Base \rightarrow Percent = 18 \div 30 = 0.6 = 60\%$ **40 *is* 20% *of what number?*** Use the following formula: $Base = Part \div Percent \rightarrow Base = 40 \div 0.20 = 200$ 40 is 20% of 200.

Your Turn!		
1) What is 25 percent of 800? 　　　200	2) 26 is what percent of 200? 13%
3) 60 is 5 percent of what number? 1,200	4) 48 is what percent of 300? 16%
5) 84 is 28 percent of what number? 300	6) 63 is what percent of 700? 9%
7) 96 is 24 percent of what number? 400	8) 40 is what percent of 800? 5%

Name: ....   **Date:** ....

Topic	Percent of Increase and Decrease

Notes	<ul><li>Percent of change (increase or decrease) is a mathematical concept that represents the degree of change over time.</li><li>To find the percentage of increase or decrease: 1- New Number – Original Number 2- The result ÷ Original Number × 100</li></ul> Or use this formula: Percent of change = $\frac{new\ number\ -\ original\ number}{original\ number} \times 100$
Example	The price of a printer increases from \$40 to \$50. What is the percent increase? **Solution:** Percent of change $= \frac{new\ number\ -\ original\ number}{original\ number} \times 100 = \frac{50\ -\ 40}{40} \times 100 = 25$ The percentage increase is 25. It means that the price of the printer increased 25%.
Your Turn!	1) In a class, the number of students has been increased from 32 to 36. What is the percentage increase? _____ % 2) The price of gasoline rose from \$4.50 to \$5.40 in one month. By what percent did the gas price rise? _____ % 3) A shirt was originally priced at \$65.00. It went on sale for \$52.00. What was the percent that the shirt was discounted? _____ % 4) Jason got a raise, and his hourly wage increased from \$40 to \$52. What is the percent increase? _____ %

Name:	Date: ....

Topic	**Percent of Increase and Decrease - Answers**
Notes	✓ Percent of change (increase or decrease) is a mathematical concept that represents the degree of change over time. ✓ To find the percentage of increase or decrease: 1- New Number – Original Number 2- The result ÷ Original Number × 100 Or use this formula: Percent of change = $\frac{new\ number\ -\ original\ number}{original\ number} \times 100$
Example	The price of a printer increases from \$40 to \$50. What is the percent increase? **Solution:** Percent of change = $\frac{new\ number\ -\ original\ number}{original\ num} \times 100 = \frac{50-40}{40} \times 100 = 25$ The percentage increase is 25. It means that the price of the printer increased 25%.
Your Turn!	1) In a class, the number of students has been increased from 32 to36. What is the percentage increase? 12.5% 2) The price of gasoline rose from \$4.50 to \$5.40 in one month. By what percent did the gas price rise? 20% 3) A shirt was originally priced at \$65.00. It went on sale for \$52.00. What was the percent that the shirt was discounted? 20% 4) Jason got a raise, and his hourly wage increased from \$40 to \$52. What is the percent increase? 30%

Name:	Date: ....

Topic	**Discount, Tax and Tip**	
Notes	✓ Discount = Multiply the regular price by the rate of discount ✓ Selling price = original price – discount ✓ To find tax, multiply the tax rate to the taxable amount (income, property value, etc.) ✓ To find tip, multiply the rate to the selling price.	
Example	The original price of a table is $300 and the tax rate is 6%. What is the final price of the table? **Solution:** First find the tax amount. To find tax: Multiply the tax rate to the taxable amount. Tax rate is 6% or 0.06. Then: $0.06 \times 300 = 18$. The tax amount is $18. Final price is: $300 + \$18 = \$318$	
Your Turn!	1) Original price of a chair: $300 Tax: 15%, Selling price: _____	2) Original price of a computer: $750 Discount: 20%, Selling price: _____
	3) Original price of a printer: $250 Tax: 10%, Selling price: _____	4) Original price of a sofa: $620 Discount: 25%, Selling price: _____
	5) Original price of a mattress: $800 Tax: 12%, Selling price: _____	6) Original price of a book: $150 Discount: 60%, Selling price: _____
	7) Restaurant bill: $35.00 Tip: 20%, Final amount: _____	8) Restaurant bill: $60.00 Tip: 25%, Final amount: _____

SHSAT Math Study Guide

| Name: .... | Date: .... |

Topic	**Discount, Tax and Tip - Answers**
Notes	✓ Discount = Multiply the regular price by the rate of discount ✓ Selling price = original price – discount ✓ To find tax, multiply the tax rate to the taxable amount (income, property value, etc.) ✓ To find tip, multiply the rate to the selling price.
Example	*The original price of a table is $300 and the tax rate is 6%. What is the final price of the table?* **Solution:** First find the tax amount. To find tax: Multiply the tax rate to the taxable amount. Tax rate is 6% or 0.06. Then: $0.06 \times 300 = 18$. The tax amount is $18. Final price is: $300 + \$18 = \$318$

Your Turn!

1) Original price of a chair: $300 Tax: 15%, Selling price: $345	2) Original price of a computer: $750 Discount: 20%, Selling price: $600
3) Original price of a printer: $250 Tax: 10%, Selling price: $275	4) Original price of a sofa: $620 Discount: 25%, Selling price: $465
5) Original price of a mattress: $800 Tax: 12%, Selling price: $896	6) Original price of a book: $150 Discount: 60%, Selling price: $60
7) Restaurant bill: $35.00 Tip: 20%, Final amount: $42	8) Restaurant bill: $60.00 Tip: 25%, Final amount: $75

Name: .... **Date:** ....

Topic	Simple Interest
Notes	✓ Simple Interest: The charge for borrowing money or the return for lending it. To solve a simple interest problem, use this formula: Interest = principal x rate x time $\Rightarrow$ $I = p \times r \times t$
Example	**Find simple interest for $3,000 investment at 5% for 4 years.** **Solution:** Use Interest formula: $I = prt$ ($P = \$3,000$, r $= 5\% = 0.05$ and $t = 4$) Then: $I = 3,000 \times 0.05 \times 4 = \$600$

Your Turn!

1) $250 at 4% for 3 years.
   Simple interest: $_____

2) $3,300 at 5% for 6 years.
   Simple interest: $_____

3) $720 at 2% for 5 years.
   Simple interest: $_____

4) $2,200 at 8% for 4 years.
   Simple interest: $_____

5) $1,800 at 3% for 2 years.
   Simple interest: $_____

6) $530 at 4% for 5 years.
   Simple interest: $_____

7) $7,000 at 5% for 3 months.
   Simple interest: $_____

8) $880 at 5% for 9 months.
   Simple interest: $_____

Name:	Date: ....

Topic	**Simple Interest - Answers**
Notes	✓ Simple Interest: The charge for borrowing money or the return for lending it. To solve a simple interest problem, use this formula: Interest = principal x rate x time $\Rightarrow I = p \times r \times t$
Example	**Find simple interest for** $3,000$ **investment at** 5% **for 4 years.** **Solution:** Use Interest formula: $I = prt$ ($P = \$3{,}000$, r = 5\% = 0.05 and $t = 4$) Then: $I = 3{,}000 \times 0.05 \times 4 = \$600$
Your Turn!	1) $250 at 4% for 3 years. Simple interest: $30 3) $720 at 2% for 5 years. Simple interest: $72 5) $1,800 at 3% for 2 years. Simple interest: $108 7) $7,000 at 5% for 3 months. Simple interest: $87.50

2) $3,300 at 5% for 6 years.
Simple interest: $990

4) $2,200 at 8% for 4 years.
Simple interest: $704

6) $530 at 4% for 5 years.
Simple interest: $106

8) $880 at 5% for 9 months.
Simple interest: $33

Name:	Date: ....

Topic	**Simplifying Variable Expressions**	
Notes	✓ In algebra, a variable is a letter used to stand for a number. The most common letters are: $x, y, z, a, b, c, m, and\ n$. ✓ Algebraic expression is an expression contains integers, variables, and the math operations such as addition, subtraction, multiplication, division, etc. ✓ In an expression, we can combine "like" terms. (values with same variable and same power)	
Example	***Simplify this expression***. $(6x + 8x + 9) =?$ Combine like terms. Then: $(6x + 8x + 4) = 14x + 9$ **(remember you cannot combine variables and numbers).**	
Your Turn!	1) $5x + 2 - 2x =$	2) $4 + 7x + 3x =$
	3) $8x + 3 - 3x =$	4) $-2 - x^2 - 6x^2 =$
	5) $3 + 10x^2 + 2 =$	6) $8x^2 + 6x + 7x^2 =$
	7) $5x^2 - 12x^2 + 8x =$	8) $2x^2 - 2x - x + 5x^2 =$
	9) $4x - (12 - 30x) =$	10) $10x - (80x - 48) =$

| Name: .... | Date: .... |

Topic	**Simplifying Variable Expressions - Answers**
Notes	✓ In algebra, a variable is a letter used to stand for a number. The most common letters are: $x, y, z, a, b, c, m,$ and n. ✓ Algebraic expression is an expression contains integers, variables, and the math operations such as addition, subtraction, multiplication, division, etc. ✓ In an expression, we can combine "like" terms. (values with same variable and same power)
Example	**Simplify this expression**. $(6x + 8x + 9) = ?$ Combine like terms. Then: $(6x + 8x + 4) = 14x + 9$ **(remember you cannot combine variables and numbers).**

Your Turn!	1) $5x + 2 - 2x =$ $\qquad 3x + 2$	2) $4 + 7x + 3x =$ $\qquad 10x + 4$
	3) $8x + 3 - 3x =$ $\qquad 5x + 3$	4) $-2 - x^2 - 6x^2 =$ $\qquad -7x^2 - 2$
	5) $3 + 10x^2 + 2 =$ $\qquad 10x^2 + 5$	6) $8x^2 + 6x + 7x^2 =$ $\qquad 15x^2 + 6x$
	7) $5x^2 - 12x^2 + 8x =$ $\qquad -7x^2 + 8x$	8) $2x^2 - 2x - x + 5x^2 =$ $\qquad 72x^2 - 3x$
	9) $4x - (12 - 30x) =$ $\qquad 34x - 12$	10) $\quad 10x - (80x - 48) =$ $\qquad -70x - 48$

Name:	Date: ....

Topic	**Simplifying Polynomial Expressions**
Notes	✓ In mathematics, a polynomial is an expression consisting of variables and coefficients that involves only the operations of addition, subtraction, multiplication, and non–negative integer exponents of variables. $$P(x) = a_n x^n + a_{n-1} x^{n-1} + \ldots + a_2 x^2 + a_1 x + a_0$$
Example	*Simplify this expression.* $(2x^2 - x^4) - (4x^4 - x^2) =$ First use distributive property: → multiply $(-)$ into $(4x^4 - x^2)$ $(2x^2 - x^4) - (4x^4 - x^2) = 2x^2 - x^4 - 4x^4 + x^2$ Then combine "like" terms: $2x^2 - x^4 - 4x^4 + x^2 = 3x^2 - 5x^4$ And write in standard form: $3x^2 - 5x^4 = -5x^4 + 3x^2$

Your Turn!	1) $(2x^3 + 5x^2) - (12x + 2x^2) =$	2) $(2x^5 + 2x^3) - (7x^3 + 6x^2) =$
	3) $(12x^4 + 4x^2) - (2x^2 - 6x^4) =$	4) $14x - 3x^2 - 2(6x^2 + 6x^3) =$
	5) $(5x^3 - 3) + 5(2x^2 - 3x^3) =$	6) $(4x^3 - 2x) - 2(4x^3 - 2x^4) =$
	7) $2(4x - 3x^3) - 3(3x^3 + 4x^2) =$	8) $(2x^2 - 2x) - (2x^3 + 5x^2) =$

Name:	Date: ....

Topic	**Simplifying Polynomial Expressions - Answers**	
Notes	✓ In mathematics, a polynomial is an expression consisting of variables and coefficients that involves only the operations of addition, subtraction, multiplication, and non–negative integer exponents of variables. $$P(x) = a_n x^n + a_{n-1} x^{n-1} + \; ... \; + a_2 x^2 + a_1 x + a_0$$	
Example	**Simplify this expression.** $(2x^2 - x^4) - (4x^4 - x^2) =$ First use distributive property: → multiply $(-)$ into $(4x^4 - x^2)$ $(2x^2 - x^4) - (4x^4 - x^2) = 2x^2 - x^4 - 4x^4 + x^2$ Then combine "like" terms: $2x^2 - x^4 - 4x^4 + x^2 = 3x^2 - 5x^4$ And write in standard form: $3x^2 - 5x^4 = -5x^4 + 3x^2$	
Your Turn!	1) $(2x^3 + 5x^2) - (12x + 2x^2) =$ $2x^3 + 3x^2 - 12x$	2) $(2x^5 + 2x^3) - (7x^3 + 6x^2) =$ $2x^5 - 5x^3 - 6x^2$
	3) $(12x^4 + 4x^2) - (2x^2 - 6x^4) =$ $18x^4 + 2x^2$	4) $14x - 3x^2 - 2(6x^2 + 6x^3) =$ $-12x^3 - 15x^2 + 14x$
	5) $(5x^3 - 3) + 5(2x^2 - 3x^3) =$ $-10x^3 + 10x^2 - 3$	6) $(4x^3 - 2x) - 2(4x^3 - 2x^4) =$ $4x^4 - 4x^3 - 2$
	7) $2(4x - 3x^3) - 3(3x^3 + 4x^2) =$ $-15x^3 - 12x^2 + 8x$	8) $(2x^2 - 2x) - (2x^3 + 5x^2) =$ $-2x^3 - 3x^2 - 2x$

| Name: .... | Date: .... |

Topic	**Evaluating One Variable**
Notes	✓ To evaluate one variable expression, find the variable and substitute a number for that variable. ✓ Perform the arithmetic operations.
Example	*Find the value of this expression for* $x = -3$. $-3x - 13$ **Solution:** Substitute -3 for x, then: $-3x - 13 = -3(-3) - 13 = 9 - 13 = -4$

1) $x = -3 \Rightarrow 3x + 8 =$ _____	2) $x = 4 \Rightarrow 4(2x + 6) =$ _____
3) $x = -1 \Rightarrow 6x + 4 =$ _____	4) $x = 7 \Rightarrow 6(5x + 3) =$ _____
5) $x = 4 \Rightarrow 5(3x + 2) =$ ___	6) $x = 6 \Rightarrow 3(2x + 4) =$ _____
7) $x = 3 \Rightarrow 7(3x + 1) =$ ___	8) $x = 8 \Rightarrow 3(3x + 7) =$ _____
9) $x = 9 \Rightarrow 2(x + 9) =$ _____	10) $x = 7 \Rightarrow 2(4x + 5) =$ _____

Your Turn!

Name:	Date: ....

Topic	**Evaluating One Variable - Answers**
Notes	✓ To evaluate one variable expression, find the variable and substitute a number for that variable. ✓ Perform the arithmetic operations.
Example	**Find the value of this expression for** $x = -3$. $\quad -3x - 13$ **Solution:** Substitute -3 for x, then: $-3x - 13 = -3(-3) - 13 = 9 - 13 = -4$

Your Turn!	1) $x = -3 \Rightarrow 3x + 8 = -1$	2) $x = 4 \Rightarrow 4(2x + 6) = 56$
	3) $x = -1 \Rightarrow 6x + 4 = -2$	4) $x = 7 \Rightarrow 6(5x + 3) = 228$
	5) $x = 4 \Rightarrow 5(3x + 2) = 70$	6) $x = 6 \Rightarrow 3(2x + 4) = 48$
	7) $x = 3 \Rightarrow 7(3x + 1) = 70$	8) $x = 8 \Rightarrow 3(3x + 7) = 93$
	9) $x = 9 \Rightarrow 2(x + 9) = 36$	10) $x = 7 \Rightarrow 2(4x + 5) = 66$

Name:	Date: ....

Topic	**Evaluating Two Variables**	
Notes	✓ To evaluate an algebraic expression, substitute a number for each variable. ✓ Perform the arithmetic operations to find the value of the expression.	
Example	***Evaluate this expression for*** $a = 4$ ***and*** $b = -2$. $\;\; 5a - 6b$ **Solution:** Substitute 4 for a, and -2 for b, then: $\qquad 5a - 6b = 5(4) - 6(-2) = 20 + 12 = 32$	
Your Turn!	1) $-4a + 6b$, $a = 4$, $b = 3$ _____	2) $5x + 3y$, $x = 2$, $y = -1$ _____
	3) $-5a + 3b$, $a = 2$, $b = -2$ _____	4) $3x - 4y$, $x = 6$, $y = 2$ _____
	5) $2z + 14 + 6k$, $z = 5$, $\qquad k = 3$ _____	6) $7a - (9 - 3b)$, $a = 1$, $\qquad\qquad b = 1$ _____
	7) $-6a + 3b$, $a = 4$, $b = 3$ _____	8) $-2a + b$, $a = 6$, $b = 9$ _____
	9) $8x + 2y$, $x = 4$, $y = 5$ _____	10) $z + 4 + 2k$, $z = 7$, $k = 4$ _____

     www.EffortlessMath.com

Name:	Date: ....

Topic	**Evaluating Two Variables - Answers**	
Notes	✓ To evaluate an algebraic expression, substitute a number for each variable. ✓ Perform the arithmetic operations to find the value of the expression.	
Example	*Evaluate this expression for* $a = 4$ *and* $b = -2$. $\quad 5a - 6b$ **Solution:** Substitute 4 for a, and -2 for b, then: $\qquad 5a - 6b = 5(4) - 6(-2) = 20 + 12 = 32$	
Your Turn!	1) $-4a + 6b$, $a = 4$, $b = 3$ $\quad 2$	2) $5x + 3y$, $x = 2$, $y = -1$ $\quad 7$
	3) $-5a + 3b$, $a = 2$, $b = -2$ -16	4) $3x - 4y$, $x = 6$, $y = 2$ $\quad 10$
	5) $2z + 14 + 6k$, $z = 5$, $\qquad k = 3$ $\quad 42$	6) $7a - (9 - 3b)$, $a = 1$, $\qquad b = 1$ $\quad 1$
	7) $-6a + 3b$, $a = 4$, $b = 3$ -15	8) $-2a + b$, $a = 6$, $b = 9$ $\quad -3$
	9) $8x + 2y$, $x = 4$, $y = 5$ $\quad 42$	10) $z + 4 + 2k$, $z = 7$, $k = 4$ $\quad 19$

Name:	Date: ....

Topic	**The Distributive Property**
Notes	✓ The distributive property (or the distributive property of multiplication over addition and subtraction) simplifies and solves expressions in the form of: $a(b + c)$ or $a(b - c)$ ✓ Distributive Property rule: $$a(b + c) = ab + ac$$
Example	***Simply***. $(5)(2x - 8)$ **Solution:** Use Distributive Property rule: $a(b + c) = ab + ac$ $(5)(2x - 8) = (5 \times 2x) + (5) \times (-8) = 10x - 40$

Your Turn!	1) $(-2)(4 - 3x) =$	2) $(6 - 3x)(-7)$
	3) $6(5 - 9x) =$	4) $10(3 - 5x) =$
	5) $5(6 - 5x) =$	6) $(-2)(-5x + 3) =$
	7) $(8 - 9x)(5) =$	8) $(-16x + 15)(-3) =$
	9) $(-2x + 7)(3) =$	10) $(-18x + 25)(-2) =$

| Name: .... | Date: .... |

Topic	**The Distributive Property - Answers**
Notes	✓ The distributive property (or the distributive property of multiplication over addition and subtraction) simplifies and solves expressions in the form of: $a(b + c)$ or $a(b - c)$ ✓ Distributive Property rule: $$a(b + c) = ab + ac$$
Example	**Simply.** $(5)(2x - 8)$ **Solution:** Use Distributive Property rule: $a(b + c) = ab + ac$ $(5)(2x - 8) = (5 \times 2x) + (5) \times (-8) = 10x - 40$

Your Turn!	1) $(-2)(4 - 3x) = 6x - 8$	2) $(6 - 3x)(-7) = 21x - 42$
	3) $6(5 - 9x) = -54x + 30$	4) $10(3 - 5x) = -50x + 30$
	5) $5(6 - 5x) = -25x + 30$	6) $(-2)(-5x + 3) = 10x - 6$
	7) $(8 - 9x)(5) = -45x + 40$	8) $(-16x + 15)(-3) =$ $48x - 45$
	9) $(-2x + 7)(3) = -6x + 21$	10) $(-18x + 25)(-2) =$ $36x - 50$

Name: ....   **Date:** ....

Topic	One–Step Equations

Notes	✓ You only need to perform one Math operation in order to solve the one-step equations.
	 ✓ To solve one-step equation, find the inverse (opposite) operation is being performed.
	 ✓ The inverse operations are:
	      - Addition and subtraction
	      - Multiplication and division

Example	***Solve this equation.*** $x + 42 = 60 \Rightarrow x = ?$ Here, the operation is addition and its inverse operation is subtraction. To solve this equation, subtract 42 from both sides of the *equation:* $x + 42 - 42 = 60 - 42$ Then simplify: $x + 42 - 42 = 60 - 42 \Rightarrow x = 18$
Your Turn!	1) $x - 15 = 36 \Rightarrow x =$ ____ 2) $18 = 13 + x \Rightarrow x =$ ____ 3) $x - 22 = 54 \Rightarrow x =$ ____ 4) $x + 14 = 24 \Rightarrow x =$ ____ 5) $4x = 24 \Rightarrow x =$ ____ 6) $\frac{x}{6} = -3 \Rightarrow x =$ ____ 7) $99 = 11x \Rightarrow x =$ ____ 8) $\frac{x}{12} = 6 \Rightarrow x =$ ____

Name:	Date: ....

Topic	One–Step Equations - Answers
Notes	✓ You only need to perform one Math operation in order to solve the one-step equations. ✓ To solve one-step equation, find the inverse (opposite) operation is being performed. ✓ The inverse operations are: - Addition and subtraction - Multiplication and division
Example	**Solve this equation.** $x + 42 = 60 \Rightarrow x = ?$ Here, the operation is addition and its inverse operation is subtraction. To solve this equation, subtract 42 from both sides of the *equation:* $x + 42 - 42 = 60 - 42$ Then simplify: $x + 42 - 42 = 60 - 42 \Rightarrow x = 18$

Your Turn!	1) $x - 15 = 36 \Rightarrow x = 51$	2) $18 = 13 + x \Rightarrow x = 5$
	3) $x - 22 = 54 \Rightarrow x = 76$	4) $x + 14 = 24 \Rightarrow x = 10$
	5) $4x = 24 \Rightarrow x = 6$	6) $\frac{x}{6} = -3 \Rightarrow x = -18$
	7) $99 = 11x \Rightarrow x = 9$	8) $\frac{x}{12} = 6 \Rightarrow x = 72$

Name: ....   **Date:** ....

Topic	Multi –Step Equations - Answers
Notes	✓ Combine "like" terms on one side. ✓ Bring variables to one side by adding or subtracting. ✓ Simplify using the inverse of addition or subtraction. ✓ Simplify further by using the inverse of multiplication or division. ✓ Check your solution by plugging the value of the variable into the original equation.
Example	**Solve this equation for** x. $\quad 2x - 3 = 13$ **Solution:** The inverse of subtraction is addition. Add 3 to both sides of the equation. Then: $2x - 3 = 13 \Rightarrow 2x - 3 = 13 + 3$ $\Rightarrow 2x = 16$. Now, divide both sides by 2, then: $\frac{2x}{2} = \frac{16}{2} \Rightarrow x = 8$ Now, check the solution: $x = 8 \Rightarrow 2x - 3 = 13 \Rightarrow 2(8) - 3 = 13 \Rightarrow 16 - 3 = 13 \qquad$ The answer $x = 8$ is correct.

Your Turn!		
	1) $4x - 12 = 8 \Rightarrow x =$	2) $12 - 3x = -6 + 3x \Rightarrow x =$
	3) $3(4 - 2x) = 24 \Rightarrow x =$	4) $15 + 5x = -7 - 6x \Rightarrow x =$
	5) $-2(5 + x) = 2 \Rightarrow x =$	6) $12 - 2x = -3 - 5x \Rightarrow x =$
	7) $14 = -(x - 9) \Rightarrow x =$	8) $11 - 4x = -4 - 3x \Rightarrow x =$

Name:	Date: ....

Topic	**Multi –Step Equations - Answers**	
Notes	✓ Combine "like" terms on one side. ✓ Bring variables to one side by adding or subtracting. ✓ Simplify using the inverse of addition or subtraction. ✓ Simplify further by using the inverse of multiplication or division. ✓ Check your solution by plugging the value of the variable into the original equation.	
Example	**Solve this equation for** x. $\ 2x - 3 = 13$ **Solution:** The inverse of subtraction is addition. Add 3 to both sides of the equation. Then: $2x - 3 = 13 \Rightarrow 2x - 3 = 13 + 3$ $\Rightarrow 2x = 16$. Now, divide both sides by 2, then: $\frac{2x}{2} = \frac{16}{2} \Rightarrow x = 8$ Now, check the solution: $x = 8 \Rightarrow 2x - 3 = 13 \Rightarrow 2(8) - 3 = 13 \Rightarrow 16 - 3 = 13$ The answer $x = 8$ is correct.	
Your Turn!	1) $4x - 12 = 8 \Rightarrow x = 5$	2) $12 - 3x = -6 + 3x \Rightarrow x = 3$
	3) $3(4 - 2x) = 24 \Rightarrow x = -2$	4) $15 + 5x = -7 - 6x \Rightarrow x = -2$
	5) $-2(5 + x) = 2 \Rightarrow x = -6$	6) $12 - 2x = -3 - 5x \Rightarrow x = -5$
	7) $14 = -(x - 9) \Rightarrow x = -5$	8) $11 - 4x = -4 - 3x \Rightarrow x = 15$

Name:	**Date:** ....

Topic	**System of Equations**

| Notes | ✓ A system of equations contains two equations and two variables. For example, consider the system of equations: $x - 2y = -2, x + 2y = 10$
✓ The easiest way to solve a system of equation is using the elimination method. The elimination method uses the addition property of equality. You can add the same value to each side of an equation.
✓ For the first equation above, you can add $x + 2y$ to the left side and 10 to the right side of the first equation: $x - 2y + (x + 2y) = -2 + 10$. Now, if you simplify, you get: $x - 2y + (x + 2y) = -2 + 10 \rightarrow 2x = 8 \rightarrow x = 4$. Now, substitute 4 for the x in the first equation: $4 - 2y = -2$. By solving this equation, $y = 3$ |

| Example | What is the value of x and y in this system of equations? $\begin{cases} 3x - y = 7 \\ -x + 4y = 5 \end{cases}$

Solution: Solving System of Equations by Elimination: $\begin{array}{l} 3x - y = 7 \\ \underline{-x + 4y = 5} \end{array}$

Multiply the second equation by 3, then add it to the first equation.

$\begin{array}{l} 3x - y = 7 \\ 3(-x + 4y = 5) \end{array} \Rightarrow \begin{array}{l} 3x - y = 7 \\ \underline{-3x + 12y = 15)} \end{array} \Rightarrow 11y = 22 \Rightarrow y = 2.$ Now, substitute 2 for y in the first equation and solve for x.

$3x - (2) = 7 \Rightarrow 3x = 9 \Rightarrow x = 3$ |

| Your Turn! | 1) $-4x + 4y = 8$
$\quad -4x + 2y = 6$

$x = $ ____
$\qquad y = $ ____

3) $y = -2$
$\quad 4x - 3y = 8$

$x = $ ____
$\qquad y = $ ____

5) $20x - 18y = -26$
$\quad -10x + 6y = 22$

$x = $ ____
$\qquad y = $ ____ | 2) $-5x + y = -3$
$\quad 3x - 8y = 24$

$x = $ ____
$\qquad y = $ ____

4) $y = -3x + 5$
$\quad 5x - 4y = -3$

$x = $ ____
$\qquad y = $ ____

6) $-9x - 12y = 15$
$\quad 2x - 6y = 14$

$x = $ ____
$\qquad y = $ ____ |

Name:	Date: ....

Topic	System of Equations- Answers
Notes	✓ A system of equations contains two equations and two variables. For example, consider the system of equations: $x - 2y = -2, x + 2y = 10$ ✓ The easiest way to solve a system of equation is using the elimination method. The elimination method uses the addition property of equality. You can add the same value to each side of an equation. ✓ For the first equation above, you can add $x + 2y$ to the left side and 10 to the right side of the first equation: $x - 2y + (x + 2y) = -2 + 10$. Now, if you simplify, you get: $x - 2y + (x + 2y) = -2 + 10 \rightarrow 2x = 8 \rightarrow x = 4$. Now, substitute 4 for the x in the first equation: $4 - 2y = -2$. By solving this equation, $y = 3$
Example	What is the value of x and y in this system of equations? $\begin{cases} 3x - y = 7 \\ -x + 4y = 5 \end{cases}$ **Solution:** Solving System of Equations by Elimination: $\begin{array}{l} 3x - y = 7 \\ \underline{-x + 4y = 5} \end{array}$ Multiply the second equation by 3, then add it to the first equation. $\begin{array}{l} 3x - y = 7 \\ \underline{3(-x + 4y = 5)} \end{array} \Rightarrow \begin{array}{l} 3x - y = 7 \\ \underline{-3x + 12y = 15} \end{array} \Rightarrow 11y = 22 \Rightarrow y = 2$. Now, substitute 2 for y in the first equation and solve for x. $3x - (2) = 7 \Rightarrow 3x = 9 \Rightarrow x = 3$
Your Turn!	1) $-4x + 4y = 8$ $-4x + 2y = 6$ $x = -1$ $\qquad y = 1$ 2) $-5x + y = -3$ $3x - 8y = 24$ $x = 0$ $\qquad y = -3$ 3) $y = -2$ $4x - 3y = 8$ $x = \dfrac{1}{2}$ $\qquad y = -2$ 4) $y = -3x + 5$ $5x - 4y = -3$ $x = 1$ $\qquad y = 2$ 5) $20x - 18y = -26$ $-10x + 6y = 22$ $x = -4$ $\qquad y = -3$ 6) $-9x - 12y = 15$ $2x - 6y = 14$ $x = 1$ $\qquad y = -2$

| **Name:** .... | **Date:** .... |

Topic	**Graphing Single–Variable Inequalities**
Notes	✓ An inequality compares two expressions using an inequality sign. ✓ Inequality signs are: "less than" $<$, "greater than" $>$, "less than or equal to" $\leq$, and "greater than or equal to" $\geq$. ✓ To graph a single–variable inequality, find the value of the inequality on the number line. ✓ For less than ($<$) or greater than ($>$) draw open circle on the value of the variable. If there is an equal sign too, then use filled circle. ✓ Draw an arrow to the right for greater or to the left for less than.
Example	*Draw a graph for this inequality.* $x < 5$ **Solution:** Since, the variable is less than 5, then we need to find 5 in the number lin and draw an open circle on it. Then, draw an arrow to the left. $\longleftarrow \overset{}{\underset{-6\;\;-5\;\;-4\;\;-3\;\;-2\;\;-1\;\;0\;\;1\;\;2\;\;3\;\;4\;\;5\;\;6}{\longleftarrow\!\!-\!\!-\!\!-\!\!-\!\!\circ}}$
Your Turn!	1) $x < 4$ $\xleftarrow{}\underset{-6\;-5\;-4\;-3\;-2\;-1\;0\;1\;2\;3\;4\;5\;6}{\vert\vert\vert\vert\vert\vert\vert\vert\vert\vert\vert\vert\vert}\xrightarrow{}$ 2) $x \geq -1$ $\xleftarrow{}\underset{-6\;-5\;-4\;-3\;-2\;-1\;0\;1\;2\;3\;4\;5\;6}{\vert\vert\vert\vert\vert\vert\vert\vert\vert\vert\vert\vert\vert}\xrightarrow{}$

1) $x < 4$

2) $x \geq -1$

3) $x \geq -3$

4) $x \leq 6$

5) $x > -6$

6) $2 > x$

7) $-2 \leq x$

8) $x > 0$

| Name: .... | Date: .... |

Topic	**Graphing Single–Variable Inequalities- Answers**
Notes	✓ An inequality compares two expressions using an inequality sign. ✓ Inequality signs are: "less than" $<$, "greater than" $>$, "less than or equal to" $\leq$, and "greater than or equal to" $\geq$. ✓ To graph a single–variable inequality, find the value of the inequality on the number line. ✓ For less than ($<$) or greater than ($>$) draw open circle on the value of the variable. If there is an equal sign too, then use filled circle. ✓ Draw an arrow to the right for greater or to the left for less than.
Example	***Draw a graph for this inequality.*** $x < 5$ **Solution:** Since, the variable is less than 5, then we need to find 5 in the number line and draw an open circle on it. Then, draw an arrow to the left.
Your Turn!	1) $x < 4$ 2) $x \geq -1$ 3) $x \geq -3$ 4) $x \leq 6$ 5) $x > -6$ 6) $2 > x$ 7) $-2 \leq x$ 8) $x > 0$

Name:	Date: ....

Topic	**One–Step Inequalities**
Notes	✓ Inequality signs are: "less than" <, "greater than" >, "less than or equal to" ≤, and "greater than or equal to" ≥. ✓ You only need to perform one Math operation in order to solve the one-step inequalities. ✓ To solve one-step inequalities, find the inverse (opposite) operation is being performed. ✓ For dividing or multiplying both sides by negative numbers, flip the direction of the inequality sign.
Example	**Solve this inequality.** $x + 12 < 60 \Rightarrow$ _____ Here, the operation is addition and its inverse operation is subtraction. To solve this inequality, subtract 12 from both sides of the **inequality:** $x + 12 - 12 < 60 - 12$ Then simplify: $x < 48$

Your Turn!	1) $4x < -8 \Rightarrow$ _____	2) $x + 6 > 28 \Rightarrow$ _____
	3) $-3x \geq 36 \Rightarrow$ _____	4) $x - 16 \leq 4 \Rightarrow$ _____
	5) $\frac{x}{2} \geq -9 \Rightarrow$ _____	6) $48 < 6x \Rightarrow$ _____
	7) $77 \leq 11x \Rightarrow$ _____	8) $\frac{x}{4} > 9 \Rightarrow$ _____

Name: ....

Date: ....

Topic	One–Step Inequalities - Answers	
Notes	✓ Inequality signs are: "less than" $<$, "greater than" $>$, "less than or equal to" $\leq$, and "greater than or equal to" $\geq$. ✓ You only need to perform one Math operation in order to solve the one-step inequalities. ✓ To solve one-step inequalities, find the inverse (opposite) operation is being performed. ✓ For dividing or multiplying both sides by negative numbers, flip the direction of the inequality sign.	
Example	**Solve this inequality.** $x + 12 < 60 \Rightarrow$ _____ Here, the operation is addition and its inverse operation is subtraction. To solve this inequality, subtract 12 from both sides of the **inequality:** $x + 12 - 12 < 60 - 12$ Then simplify: $x < 48$	
Your Turn!	1) $4x < -8 \Rightarrow x < -2$	2) $x + 6 > 28 \Rightarrow x > 22$
	3) $-3x \geq 36 \Rightarrow x \leq -12$	4) $x - 16 \leq 4 \Rightarrow x \leq 20$
	5) $\frac{x}{2} \geq -9 \Rightarrow x \geq -18$	6) $48 < 6x \Rightarrow 8 < x$
	7) $77 \leq 11x \Rightarrow 7 \leq x$	8) $\frac{x}{4} > 9 \Rightarrow x > 36$

Name:	Date: ....

Topic	**Multi –Step Inequalities**
Notes	✓ Isolate the variable. ✓ Simplify using the inverse of addition or subtraction. ✓ Simplify further by using the inverse of multiplication or division. ✓ For dividing or multiplying both sides by negative numbers, flip the direction of the inequality sign.
Example	***Solve this inequality.*** $3x + 12 \leq 21$ **Solution:** First subtract 12 from both sides: $3x + 12 - 12 \leq 21 - 12$ Then simplify: $3x + 12 - 12 \leq 21 - 12 \rightarrow 3x \leq 9$ Now divide both sides by 3: $\frac{3x}{3} \leq \frac{9}{3} \rightarrow x \leq 3$
Your Turn!	1) $5x + 6 < 36 \rightarrow$ _____ 2) $2x - 8 \leq 6 \rightarrow$ _____ 3) $2x - 5 \leq 17 \rightarrow$ _____ 4) $14 - 7x \geq -7 \rightarrow$ _____ 5) $18 - 6x \geq -6 \rightarrow$ _____ 6) $2x - 18 \leq 16 \rightarrow$ _____ 7) $8 + 4x < 44 \rightarrow$ _____ 8) $5 - 4x < 17 \rightarrow$ _____

Name:	Date: ....

Topic	**Multi –Step Inequalities - Answers**
Notes	✓ Isolate the variable. ✓ Simplify using the inverse of addition or subtraction. ✓ Simplify further by using the inverse of multiplication or division. ✓ For dividing or multiplying both sides by negative numbers, flip the direction of the inequality sign.
Example	*Solve this inequality*. $3x + 12 \leq 21$ **Solution:** First subtract 12 from both sides: $3x + 12 - 12 \leq 21 - 12$ Then simplify: $3x + 12 - 12 \leq 21 - 12 \rightarrow 3x \leq 9$ Now divide both sides by 3: $\frac{3x}{3} \leq \frac{9}{3} \rightarrow x \leq 3$

Your Turn!	1) $5x + 6 < 36 \rightarrow x < 6$	2) $2x - 8 \leq 6 \rightarrow x \leq 7$
	3) $2x - 5 \leq 17 \rightarrow x \leq 11$	4) $14 - 7x \geq -7 \rightarrow x \leq 3$
	5) $18 - 6x \geq -6 \rightarrow x \leq 4$	6) $2x - 18 \leq 16 \rightarrow x \leq 17$
	7) $8 + 4x < 44 \rightarrow x < 9$	8) $5 - 4x < 17 \rightarrow x > -3$

Name: .... **Date:** ....

Topic	Finding Slope
Notes	✓ The slope of a line represents the direction of a line on the coordinate plane. ✓ A line on coordinate plane can be drawn by connecting two points. ✓ To find the slope of a line, we need two points. ✓ The slope of a line with two points A (x_1, y_1) and B (x_2, y_2) can be found by using this formula: $\frac{y_2 - y_1}{x_2 - x_1} = \frac{rise}{run}$ ✓ The equation of a line is typically written as $y = mx + b$ where m is the slope and b is the y-intercept.
Examples	***Find the slope of the line through these two points:*** $(4, -12)$ *and* $(9, 8)$. **Solution:** Slope = $\frac{y_2 - y_1}{x_2 - x_1}$. Let (x_1, y_1) be $(4, -12)$ and (x_2, y_2) be $(9, 8)$. ***Then:*** slope = $\frac{y_2 - y_1}{x_2 - x_1} = \frac{8 - (-12)}{9 - 4} = \frac{8 + 12}{5} = \frac{20}{5} = 4$ ***Find the slope of the line with equation*** $y = 5x - 6$ **Solution:** when the equation of a line is written in the form of $y = mx + b$, the slope is m. In this line: $y = 5x - 6$, the slope is 5.

Your Turn!	1) $(2, 3), (4, 7)$ Slope = ____	2) $(-2, 2), (0, 4)$ Slope = ____
	3) $(4, -2), (2, 4)$ Slope = ____	4) $(-4, -1), (0, 7)$ Slope = ____
	5) $y = 3x + 18$ Slope = ____	6) $y = 12x - 3$ Slope = ____

Name: ....

Date: ....

Topic	**Finding Slope - Answers**
Notes	✓ The slope of a line represents the direction of a line on the coordinate plane. ✓ A line on coordinate plane can be drawn by connecting two points. ✓ To find the slope of a line, we need two points. ✓ The slope of a line with two points A (x_1, y_1) and B (x_2, y_2) can be found by using this formula: $\frac{y_2 - y_1}{x_2 - x_1} = \frac{rise}{run}$ ✓ The equation of a line is typically written as $y = mx + b$ where m is the slope and b is the y-intercept.
Examples	***Find the slope of the line through these two points:*** $(4, -12)$ *and* $(9, 8)$. **Solution:** Slope $= \frac{y_2 - y_1}{x_2 - x_1}$. Let (x_1, y_1) be $(4, -12)$ and (x_2, y_2) be $(9, 8)$. **Then:** slope $= \frac{y_2 - y_1}{x_2 - x_1} = \frac{8 - (-12)}{9 - 4} = \frac{8 + 12}{5} = \frac{20}{5} = 4$ ***Find the slope of the line with equation*** $y = 5x - 6$ **Solution:** when the equation of a line is written in the form of $y = mx + b$, the slope is m. In this line: $y = 5x - 6$, the slope is 5.

Your Turn!	1) $(2, 3), (4, 7)$ Slope $= 2$	2) $(-2, 2), (0, 4)$ Slope $= 1$
	3) $(4, -2), (2, 4)$ Slope $= -3$	4) $(-4, -1), (0, 7)$ Slope $= 2$
	5) $y = 3x + 18$ Slope $= 3$	6) $y = 12x - 3$ Slope $= 12$

Name:	**Date:** ....

Topic	**Graphing Lines Using Slope–Intercept Form**
Notes	✓ Slope–intercept form of a line: given the slope **m** and the **y**–intercept (the intersection of the line and y-axis) **b**, then the equation of the line is: $$y = mx + b$$
Example	***Sketch the graph of*** $y = -2x - 1$. **Solution:** To graph this line, we need to find two points. When x is zero the value of y is -1. And when y is zero the value of x is $-\frac{1}{2}$. $$x = 0 \rightarrow y = -2(0) - 1 = -1, y = 0 \rightarrow 0$$ $$= -2x - 1 \rightarrow x = -\frac{1}{2}$$ Now, we have two points: $(0, -1)$ and $(-\frac{1}{2}, 0)$. Find the points and graph the line. Remember that the slope of the line is $-\frac{1}{2}$. 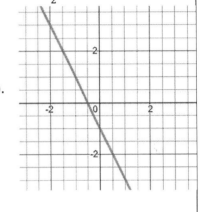
Your Turn!	1) $y = -4x + 1$ 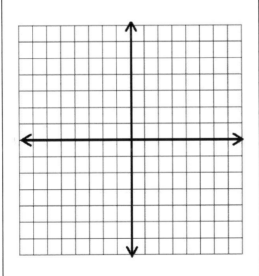 2) $y = -x - 5$ 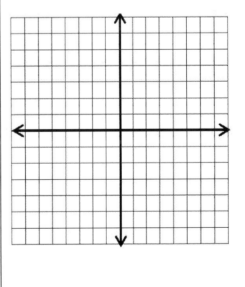

Name:	**Date:** ....

Topic	**Graphing Lines Using Slope–Intercept Form - Answers**
Notes	✓ Slope–intercept form of a line: given the slope m and the y–intercept (the intersection of the line and y-axis) b, then the equation of the line is: $$y = mx + b$$
Example	*Sketch the graph of* $y = -2x - 1$. **Solution:** To graph this line, we need to find two points. When x is zero the value of y is -1. And when y is zero the value of x is $-\frac{1}{2}$. $$x = 0 \rightarrow y = -2(0) - 1 = -1, y = 0 \rightarrow 0$$ $$= -2x - 1 \rightarrow x = -\frac{1}{2}$$ Now, we have two points: $(0, -1)$ and $(-\frac{1}{2}, 0)$. Find the points and graph the line. Remember that the slope of the line is $-\frac{1}{2}$. 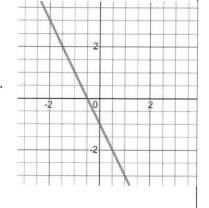
Your Turn!	1) $y = -4x + 1$ 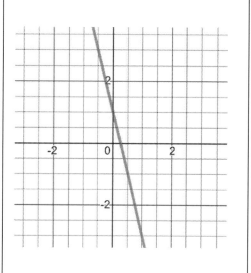 2) $y = -x - 5$ 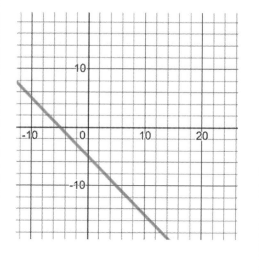

Name:	Date: ....

Topic	**Writing Linear Equations**
Notes	✓ The equation of a line: $y = mx + b$ ✓ Identify the slope. ✓ Find the y–intercept. This can be done by substituting the slope and the coordinates of a point (x, y) on the line.
Example	**Write the equation of the line through $(3, 1)$ and $(-1, 5)$.** **Solution:** $Slop = \frac{y_2 - y_1}{x_2 - x_1} = \frac{5-1}{-1-3} = \frac{4}{-4} = -1 \rightarrow m = -1$ To find the value of b, you can use either points. The answer will be the same: $y = -x + b$ $(3, 1) \rightarrow 1 = -3 + b \rightarrow b = 4$ $(-1, 5) \rightarrow 5 = -(-1) + b \rightarrow b = 4$ The equation of the line is: $y = -x + 4$

Your Turn!	1) through: $(-2, 7), (1, 4)$ $y =$	2) through: $(6, 1), (5, 2)$ $y =$
	3) through: $(5, -1), (8, 2)$ $y =$	4) through: $(-2, 4), (4, -8)$ $y =$
	5) through: $(6, -5), (-5, 6)$ $y =$	6) through: $(4, -4), (-2, 8)$ $y =$
	7) through $(8, 8)$, Slope: 2 $y =$	8) through $(-7, 10)$, Slope: -2 $y =$

Name:	Date: ....

Topic	**Writing Linear Equations - Answers**
Notes	✓ The equation of a line: $y = mx + b$ ✓ Identify the slope. ✓ Find the y–intercept. This can be done by substituting the slope and the coordinates of a point (x, y) on the line.
Example	**Write the equation of the line through** $(3, 1)$ **and** $(-1, 5)$. **Solution:** $Slop = \frac{y_2 - y_1}{x_2 - x_1} = \frac{5 - 1}{-1 - 3} = \frac{4}{-4} = -1 \rightarrow m = -1$ To find the value of b, you can use either points. The answer will be the same: $y = -x + b$ $(3, 1) \rightarrow 1 = -3 + b \rightarrow b = 4$ $(-1, 5) \rightarrow 5 = -(-1) + b \rightarrow b = 4$ The equation of the line is: $y = -x + 4$

Your Turn!	1) through: $(-2, 7), (1, 4)$ $y = -x + 5$	2) through: $(6, 1), (5, 2)$ $y = -x + 7$
	3) through: $(5, -1), (8, 2)$ $y = x - 6$	4) through: $(-2, 4), (4, -8)$ $y = -2x$
	5) through: $(6, -5), (-5, 6)$ $y = -x + 1$	6) through: $(4, -4), (-2, 8)$ $y = -2x + 4$
	7) through $(8, 8)$, Slope: 2 $y = 2x - 8$	8) through $(-7, 10)$, Slope: -2 $y = -2x - 4$

Name: ....   **Date:** ....

Topic	**Finding Midpoint**
Notes	✓ The middle of a line segment is its midpoint. ✓ The Midpoint of two endpoints A (x_1, y_1) and B (x_2, y_2) can be found using this formula: $M(\frac{x_1+x_2}{2}, \frac{y_1+y_2}{2})$
Example	Find the midpoint of the line segment with the given endpoints. $(\mathbf{1}, -\mathbf{2}), (\mathbf{3}, \mathbf{6})$ **Solution:** Midpoint $= (\frac{x_1+x_2}{2}, \frac{y_1+y_2}{2}) \rightarrow (x_1, y_1) = (1, -2)$ and $(x_2, y_2) = (3, 6)$ Midpoint $= (\frac{1+3}{2}, \frac{-2+6}{2}) \rightarrow (\frac{4}{2}, \frac{4}{2}) \rightarrow M(2, 2)$

Your Turn!	1) $(6, 0), (-4, 2)$ **Midpoint** = (__, __)	2) $(4, -1), (2, 3)$ **Midpoint** = (__, __)
	3) $(-3, 4), (-5, 0)$ **Midpoint** = (__, __)	4) $(8, 1), (-4, 5)$ **Midpoint** = (__, __)
	5) $(6, 7), (-4, 5)$ **Midpoint** = (__, __)	6) $(2, -3), (2, 5)$ **Midpoint** = (__, __)
	7) $(7, 3), (-1, -7)$ **Midpoint** = (__, __)	8) $(3, 9), (-1, 5)$ **Midpoint** = (__, __)
	9) $(3, 4), (-7, -6)$ **Midpoint** = (__, __)	10) $(-5, 2), (11, -6)$ **Midpoint** = (__, __)

| Name: .... | Date: .... |

Topic	**Finding Midpoint - Answers**
Notes	✓ The middle of a line segment is its midpoint. ✓ The Midpoint of two endpoints A (x_1, y_1) and B (x_2, y_2) can be found using this formula: $M(\frac{x_1+x_2}{2}, \frac{y_1+y_2}{2})$
Example	Find the midpoint of the line segment with the given endpoints. $(\mathbf{1}, -\mathbf{2}), (\mathbf{3}, \mathbf{6})$ **Solution:** Midpoint $= (\frac{x_1+x_2}{2}, \frac{y_1+y_2}{2}) \rightarrow (x_1, y_1) = (1, -2)$ and $(x_2, y_2) = (3, 6)$ Midpoint $= (\frac{1+3}{2}, \frac{-2+6}{2}) \rightarrow (\frac{4}{2}, \frac{4}{2}) \rightarrow M(2, 2)$

Your Turn!

1) $(6, 0), (-4, 2)$ ***Midpoint*** $= (1, 1)$	2) $(4, -1), (2, 3)$ ***Midpoint*** $= (3, 1)$
3) $(-3, 4), (-5, 0)$ ***Midpoint*** $= (-4, 2)$	4) $(8, 1), (-4, 5)$ ***Midpoint*** $= (2, 3)$
5) $(6, 7), (-4, 5)$ ***Midpoint*** $= (1, 6)$	6) $(2, -3), (2, 5)$ ***Midpoint*** $= (2, 1)$
7) $(7, 3), (-1, -7)$ ***Midpoint*** $= (3, -2)$	8) $(3, 9), (-1, 5)$ ***Midpoint*** $= (1, 7)$
9) $(3, 4), (-7, -6)$ ***Midpoint*** $= (-2, -1)$	10) $(-5, 2), (11, -6)$ ***Midpoint*** $= (3, -2)$

Name:	Date: ....

Topic	**Finding Distance of Two Points**
Notes	✓ Use this formula to find the distance of two points A (x_1, y_1) and B (x_2, y_2): $$d = \sqrt{(x_2 - x_1)^2 + (y_2 - y_1)^2}$$
Example	*Find the distance of two points* $(-1, 5)$ and $(4, -7)$. **Solution:** *Use distance of two points formula:* $d =$ $\sqrt{(x_2 - x_1)^2 + (y_2 - y_1)^2}$ $(x_1, y_1) = (-1, 5),$ and $(x_2, y_2) = (4, -7)$ Then: $d = \sqrt{(x_2 - x_1)^2 + (y_2 - y_1)^2} \rightarrow d =$ $\sqrt{(4 - (-1))^2 + (-7 - 5)^2} = \sqrt{(-5)^2 + (-12)^2} = \sqrt{25 + 144} =$ $\sqrt{169} = 13$
Your Turn!	1) $(6, 2), (-4, 2)$ **Distance** = ____ 2) $(2, -3), (2, 5)$ **Distance** = ____ 3) $(-5, 10), (7, 1)$ **Distance** = ____ 4) $(8, 1), (-4, 6)$ **Distance** = ____ 5) $(-3, 6), (-4, 5)$ **Distance** = ____ 6) $(4, -1), (14, 23)$ **Distance** = ____ 7) $(-3, 4), (-5, 0)$ **Distance** = ____ 8) $(3, 9), (-1, 5)$ **Distance** = ____

Name:	Date: ....

Topic	**Finding Distance of Two Points - Answers**	
Notes	✓ Use this formula to find the distance of two points A (x_1, y_1) and B (x_2, y_2): $$d = \sqrt{(x_2 - x_1)^2 + (y_2 - y_1)^2}$$	
Example	**Find the distance of two points** $(-1, 5)$ and $(4, -7)$. **Solution: *Use distance of two points formula:*** $d = \sqrt{(x_2 - x_1)^2 + (y_2 - y_1)^2}$ $(x_1, y_1) = (-1, 5)$, and $(x_2, y_2) = (4, -7)$ Then: $d = \sqrt{(x_2 - x_1)^2 + (y_2 - y_1)^2} \rightarrow d =$ $\sqrt{(4 - (-1))^2 + (-7 - 5)^2} = \sqrt{(-5)^2 + (-12)^2} = \sqrt{25 + 144} =$ $\sqrt{169} = 13$	
Your Turn!	1) $(6, 2), (-4, 2)$ **Distance** $= 10$	2) $(2, -3), (2, 5)$ **Distance** $= 8$
	3) $(-5, 10), (7, 1)$ **Distance** $= 15$	4) $(8, 1), (-4, 6)$ **Distance** $= 13$
	5) $(-3, 6), (-4, 5)$ **Distance** $= \sqrt{2}$	6) $(4, -1), (14, 23)$ **Distance** $= 26$
	7) $(-3, 4), (-5, 0)$ **Distance** $= \sqrt{20} = 2\sqrt{5}$	8) $(3, 9), (-1, 5)$ **Distance** $= \sqrt{32} = 4\sqrt{2}$

Name:	Date: ....

Topic	**Multiplication Property of Exponents**	
Notes	✓ Exponents are shorthand for repeated multiplication of the same number by itself. For example, instead of 2×2, we can write 2^2. For $3 \times 3 \times 3 \times 3$, we can write 3^4 ✓ In algebra, a variable is a letter used to stand for a number. The most common letters are: $x, y, z, a, b, c, m,$ and n. ✓ Exponent's rules: $x^a \times x^b = x^{a+b}$, $\frac{x^a}{x^b} = x^{a-b}$ $(x^a)^b = x^{a \times b}$ $\qquad$ $(xy)^a = x^a \times y^a$ $\qquad$ $(\frac{a}{b})^c = \frac{a^c}{b^c}$	
Example	***Multiply.*** $4x^3 \times 2x^2$ Use Exponent's rules: $x^a \times x^b = x^{a+b} \rightarrow x^3 \times x^2 = x^{3+2} = x^5$ Then: $4x^3 \times 2x^2 = 8x^5$	
Your Turn!	1) $x^2 \times 3x =$	2) $5x^4 \times x^2 =$
	3) $3x^2 \times 4x^5 =$	4) $3x^2 \times 6xy =$
	5) $3x^5y \times 5x^2y^3 =$	6) $3x^2y^2 \times 5x^2y^8 =$
	7) $5x^2y \times 5x^2y^7 =$	8) $6x^6 \times 4x^9y^4 =$
	9) $8x^2y^5 \times 7x^5y^3 =$	10) $12x^6x^2 \times 3xy^5 =$

| Name: .... | Date: .... |

Topic	**Multiplication Property of Exponents - Answers**
Notes	✓ Exponents are shorthand for repeated multiplication of the same number by itself. For example, instead of 2×2, we can write 2^2. For $3 \times 3 \times 3 \times 3$, we can write 3^4 ✓ In algebra, a variable is a letter used to stand for a number. The most common letters are: $x, y, z, a, b, c, m,$ and n. ✓ Exponent's rules: $x^a \times x^b = x^{a+b}$, $\dfrac{x^a}{x^b} = x^{a-b}$ $\qquad (x^a)^b = x^{a \times b} \qquad\qquad (xy)^a = x^a \times y^a \qquad \left(\dfrac{a}{b}\right)^c = \dfrac{a^c}{b^c}$
Example	**Multiply.** $4x^3 \times 2x^2$ Use Exponent's rules: $x^a \times x^b = x^{a+b} \rightarrow x^3 \times x^2 = x^{3+2} = x^5$ Then: $4x^3 \times 2x^2 = 8x^5$
Your Turn!	1) $x^2 \times 3x = 3x^3$ 2) $5x^4 \times x^2 = 5x^6$ 3) $3x^2 \times 4x^5 = 12x^7$ 4) $3x^2 \times 6xy = 18x^3y$ 5) $3x^5y \times 5x^2y^3 = 15x^7y^4$ 6) $3x^2y^2 \times 5x^2y^8 = 15x^4y^{10}$ 7) $5x^2y \times 5x^2y^7 = 25x^4y^8$ 8) $6x^6 \times 4x^9y^4 = 24x^{15}y^4$ 9) $8x^2y^5 \times 7x^5y^3 = 56x^7y^8$ 10) $12x^6x^2 \times 3xy^5 = 36x^9y^5$

Name:	Date: ....

Topic	**Division Property of Exponents**
Notes	✓ For division of exponents use these formulas: $\frac{x^a}{x^b} = x^{a-b}$, $x \neq 0$ $\frac{x^a}{x^b} = \frac{1}{x^{b-a}}$, $x \neq 0$, $\qquad$ $\frac{1}{x^b} = x^{-b}$
Example	**Simplify**. $\frac{6x^3 y}{36x^2 y^3}$ First cancel the common factor: $6 \rightarrow \frac{6x^3 y}{36x^2 y^3} = \frac{x^3 y}{6x^2 y^3}$ Use Exponent's rules: $\frac{x^a}{x^b} = x^{a-b} \rightarrow \frac{x^3}{x^2} = x^{3-2} = x^1 = x$ Then: $\frac{6x^3 y}{36x^2 y^3} = \frac{xy}{9y^3} \rightarrow$ now cancel the common factor: $y \rightarrow \frac{xy}{6y^3} = \frac{x}{6y^2}$

Your Turn!	1) $\frac{3^7}{3^2} =$	2) $\frac{5x}{10x^3} =$
	3) $\frac{3x^3}{2x^5} =$	4) $\frac{12x^3}{14x^6} =$
	5) $\frac{12x^3}{9y^8} =$	6) $\frac{25xy^4}{5x^6 y^2} =$
	7) $\frac{2x^4 y^5}{7xy^2} =$	8) $\frac{16x^2 y^8}{4x^3} =$
	9) $\frac{12x^4}{15x^7 y^9} =$	10) $\frac{12yx^4}{10yx^8} =$

Name:	Date: ....

Topic	**Division Property of Exponents - Answers**
Notes	✓ For division of exponents use following formulas: $\frac{x^a}{x^b} = x^{a-b}$, $x \neq 0$ $\frac{x^a}{x^b} = \frac{1}{x^{b-a}}$, $x \neq 0$, $\qquad \frac{1}{x^b} = x^{-b}$
Example	**Simplify**. $\frac{6x^3y}{36x^2y^3}$ First cancel the common factor: $6 \rightarrow \frac{6x^3y}{36x^2y^3} = \frac{x^3y}{6x^2y^3}$ Use Exponent's rules: $\frac{x^a}{x^b} = x^{a-b} \rightarrow \frac{x^3}{x^2} = x^{3-2} = x^1 = x$ Then: $\frac{6x^3y}{36x^2y^3} = \frac{xy}{9y^3} \rightarrow$ now cancel the common factor: $y \rightarrow \frac{xy}{6y^3} = \frac{x}{6y^2}$

Your Turn!	1) $\frac{3^7}{3^2} = 3^5$	2) $\frac{5x}{10x^3} = \frac{1}{2x^2}$
	3) $\frac{3x^3}{2x^5} = \frac{3}{2x^2}$	4) $\frac{12x^3}{14x^6} = \frac{6}{7x^3}$
	5) $\frac{12x^3}{9y^8} = \frac{4x^3}{3y^8}$	6) $\frac{25xy^4}{5x^6y^2} = \frac{5y^2}{x^5}$
	7) $\frac{2x^4y^5}{7xy^2} = \frac{2x^3y^3}{7}$	8) $\frac{16x^2y^8}{4x^3} = \frac{4y^8}{x}$
	9) $\frac{12x^4}{15x^7y^9} = \frac{4}{5x^3y^9}$	10) $\frac{12y^8x^4}{10y^2x^8} = \frac{6y^6}{5x^4}$

| Name: .... | Date: .... |

Topic	**Powers of Products and Quotients**
Notes	✓ For any nonzero numbers a and b and any integer x, $$(ab)^x = a^x \times b^x, \left(\frac{a}{b}\right)^c = \frac{a^c}{b^c}$$
Example	**Simplify.** $\left(\frac{2x^3}{x}\right)^2$ First cancel the common factor: $x \to \left(\frac{2x^3}{x}\right)^2 = (2x^2)^2$ Use Exponent's rules: $(ab)^x = a^x \times b^x$ Then: $(2x^2)^2 = (2)^2 (x^2)^2 = 4x^4$
Your Turn!	1) $(4x^3 x^3)^2 =$ 2) $(3x^3 \times 5x)^2 =$ 3) $(10x^{11}y^3)^2 =$ 4) $(9x^7 y^5)^2 =$ 5) $(4x^4 y^6)^3 =$ 6) $(3x \times 4y^3)^2 =$ 7) $\left(\frac{5x}{x^2}\right)^2 =$ 8) $\left(\frac{x^4 y^4}{x^2 y^2}\right)^3 =$ 9) $\left(\frac{25x}{5x^6}\right)^2 =$ 10) $\left(\frac{x^8}{x^6 y^2}\right)^2 =$

Name:	Date: ....

Topic	**Powers of Products and Quotients - Answers**	
Notes	✓ For any nonzero numbers a and b and any integer x, $$(ab)^x = a^x \times b^x, \left(\frac{a}{b}\right)^c = \frac{a^c}{b^c}$$	
Example	**Simplify.** $\left(\frac{2x^3}{x}\right)^2$ First cancel the common factor: $x \to \left(\frac{2x^3}{x}\right)^2 = \left(2x^2\right)^2$ Use Exponent's rules: $(ab)^x = a^x \times b^x$ Then: $\left(2x^2\right)^2 = (2)^2\left(x^2\right)^2 = 4x^4$	
Your Turn!	1) $(4x^3x^3)^2 = 16x^{12}$	2) $(3x^3 \times 5x)^2 = 225x^8$
	3) $(10x^{11}y^3)^2 = 100x^{22}y^6$	4) $(9x^7y^5)^2 = 81x^{14}y^{10}$
	5) $(4x^4y^6)^3 = 64\,x^{12}y^{18}$	6) $(3x \times 4y^3)^2 = 144x^2y^6$
	7) $\left(\frac{5x}{x^2}\right)^2 = \frac{25}{x^2}$	8) $\left(\frac{x^4y^4}{x^2y^2}\right)^3 = x^6y^6$
	9) $\left(\frac{25x}{5x^6}\right)^2 = \frac{25}{x^{10}}$	10) $\left(\frac{x^8}{x^6y^2}\right)^2 = \frac{x^4}{y^4}$

Name: ....

Date: ....

Topic	Zero and Negative Exponents	
Notes	✓ A negative exponent is the reciprocal of that number with a positive exponent. $(3)^{-2} = \frac{1}{3^2}$ ✓ Zero-Exponent Rule: $a^0 = 1$, this means that anything raised to the zero power is 1. For example: $(28x^2y)^0 = 1$	
Example	***Evaluate.*** $\left(\frac{1}{3}\right)^{-2} =$ Use negative exponent's rule: $\left(\frac{1}{x^a}\right)^{-2} = (x^a)^2 \rightarrow \left(\frac{1}{3}\right)^{-2} = (3)^2 =$ Then: $(3)^2 = 9$	
Your Turn!	1) $2^{-3} =$	2) $3^{-3} =$
	3) $7^{-3} =$	4) $1^{-3} =$
	5) $8^{-3} =$	6) $4^{-4} =$
	7) $10^{-3} =$	8) $7^{-4} =$
	9) $\left(\frac{1}{8}\right)^{-1} =$	10) $\left(\frac{1}{5}\right)^{-2} =$

Name: .... Date: ....

Topic	**Zero and Negative Exponents - Answers**
Notes	✓ A negative exponent is the reciprocal of that number with a positive exponent. $(3)^{-2} = \frac{1}{3^2}$ ✓ Zero-Exponent Rule: $a^0 = 1$, this means that anything raised to the zero power is 1. For example: $(28x^2y)^0 = 1$
Example	*Evaluate.* $\left(\frac{1}{3}\right)^{-2} =$ Use negative exponent's rule: $\left(\frac{1}{x^a}\right)^{-2} = (x^a)^2 \rightarrow \left(\frac{1}{3}\right)^{-2} = (3)^2 =$ Then: $(3)^2 = 9$

Your Turn!		
	1) $2^{-3} = \frac{1}{8}$	2) $3^{-3} = \frac{1}{27}$
	3) $7^{-3} = \frac{1}{343}$	4) $1^{-3} = 1$
	5) $8^{-3} = \frac{1}{512}$	6) $4^{-4} = \frac{1}{256}$
	7) $10^{-3} = \frac{1}{1,000}$	8) $7^{-4} = \frac{1}{2,401}$
	9) $\left(\frac{1}{8}\right)^{-1} = 8$	10) $\left(\frac{1}{5}\right)^{-2} = 25$

Name:	Date: ....

Topic	**Negative Exponents and Negative Bases**	
Notes	✓ Make the power positive. A negative exponent is the reciprocal of that number with a positive exponent. ✓ The parenthesis is important! 5^{-2} is not the same as $(-5)^{-2}$ $(-5)^{-2} = -\dfrac{1}{5^2}$ and $(-5)^{-2} = +\dfrac{1}{5^2}$	
Example	**Simplify.** $\left(-\dfrac{3x}{4yz}\right)^{-2} =$ Use negative exponent's rule: $\left(\dfrac{x^a}{x^b}\right)^{-2} = \left(\dfrac{x^b}{x^a}\right)^2 \rightarrow \left(-\dfrac{3x}{4yz}\right)^{-3} = \left(-\dfrac{4yz}{3x}\right)^3$ Now use exponent's rule: $\left(\dfrac{a}{b}\right)^c = \dfrac{a^c}{b^c} \rightarrow \left(-\dfrac{4yz}{3x}\right)^3 = \dfrac{4^3 y^3 z^3}{3^3 x^3} = \dfrac{64 y^3 z^3}{27 x^3}$	
Your Turn!	1) $-5x^{-2}y^{-3} =$	2) $20x^{-4}y^{-1} =$
	3) $14a^{-6}b^{-7} =$	4) $-12x^2 y^{-3} =$
	5) $-\dfrac{25}{x^{-6}} =$	6) $\dfrac{7b}{-9c^{-4}} =$
	7) $\dfrac{7ab}{a^{-3}b^{-1}} =$	8) $-\dfrac{5n^{-2}}{10p^{-3}} = -$
	9) $\dfrac{4ab^{-2}}{-3c^{-2}} =$	10) $\left(\dfrac{3a}{2c}\right)^{-2} =$

Name:	Date: ....

Topic	**Negative Exponents and Negative Bases - Answers**
Notes	✓ Make the power positive. A negative exponent is the reciprocal of that number with a positive exponent. ✓ The parenthesis is important! ✓ 5^{-2} is not the same as $(-5)^{-2}$ $(-5)^{-2} = -\dfrac{1}{5^2}$ and $(-5)^{-2} = +\dfrac{1}{5^2}$
Example	*Simplify.* $\left(-\dfrac{3x}{4yz}\right)^{-2} =$ Use negative exponent's rule: $\left(\dfrac{x^a}{x^b}\right)^{-2} = \left(\dfrac{x^b}{x^a}\right)^2 \rightarrow \left(-\dfrac{3x}{4yz}\right)^{-3} = \left(-\dfrac{4yz}{3x}\right)^3$ Now use exponent's rule: $\left(\dfrac{a}{b}\right)^c = \dfrac{a^c}{b^c} \rightarrow \left(-\dfrac{4yz}{3x}\right)^3 = \dfrac{4^3 y^3 z^3}{3^3 x^3} = \dfrac{64 y^3 z^3}{27 x^3}$

Your Turn!	1) $-5x^{-2}y^{-3} = -\dfrac{5}{x^2 y^3}$	2) $20x^{-4}y^{-1} = \dfrac{20}{x^4 y}$
	3) $14a^{-6}b^{-7} = \dfrac{14}{a^6 b^7}$	4) $-12x^2 y^{-3} = -\dfrac{12x^2}{y^3}$
	5) $-\dfrac{25}{x^{-6}} = -25x^6$	6) $\dfrac{7b}{-9c^{-4}} = -\dfrac{7bc^4}{9}$
	7) $\dfrac{7ab}{a^{-3}b^{-1}} = 7a^4 b^2$	8) $-\dfrac{5n^{-2}}{10p^{-3}} = -\dfrac{p^3}{2n^2}$
	9) $\dfrac{4ab^{-2}}{-3c^{-2}} = -\dfrac{4ac^2}{3b^2}$	10) $\left(\dfrac{3a}{2c}\right)^{-2} = \dfrac{4c^2}{9a^2}$

Name:	Date: ....

Topic	**Scientific Notation**
Notes	✓ It is used to write very big or very small numbers in decimal form. ✓ In scientific notation all numbers are written in the form of: $m \times 10^n$ <table><tr><td>**Decimal notation**</td><td>**Scientific notation**</td></tr><tr><td>3</td><td>3×10^0</td></tr><tr><td>$-45,000$</td><td>-4.5×10^4</td></tr><tr><td>0.3</td><td>3×10^{-1}</td></tr><tr><td>2,122.456</td><td>2.122456×10^3</td></tr></table>
Example	*Write* 0.00054 *in scientific notation.* First, move the decimal point to the right so that you have a number that is between 1 and 10. Then: $m = 5.4$ Now, determine how many places the decimal moved in step 1 by the power of 10. Then: $10^{-4} \rightarrow$ When the decimal moved to the right, the exponent is negative. Then: $0.00054 = 5.4 \times 10^{-4}$
Your Turn!	1) $0.000325 =$ 2) $0.000023 =$ 3) $52,000,000 =$ 4) $21,000 =$ 5) $3 \times 10^{-1} =$ 6) $5 \times 10^{-2} =$ 7) $1.2 \times 10^3 =$ 8) $2 \times 10^{-4} =$

Name:	Date: ....

Topic	**Scientific Notation - Answers**
Notes	✓ It is used to write very big or very small numbers in decimal form. ✓ In scientific notation all numbers are written in the form of: $$m \times 10^n$$ **Decimal notation** **Scientific notation** 3 3×10^0 $-45{,}000$ -4.5×10^4 0.3 3×10^{-1} $2{,}122.456$ 2.122456×10^3
Example	*Write 0.00054 in scientific notation.* First, move the decimal point to the right so that you have a number that is between 1 and 10. Then: $m = 5.4$ Now, determine how many places the decimal moved in step 1 by the power of 10. Then: $10^{-4} \rightarrow$ When the decimal moved to the right, the exponent is negative. Then: $0.00054 = 5.4 \times 10^{-4}$

Your Turn!	1) $0.000325 = 3.25 \times 10^{-4}$	2) $0.00023 = 2.3 \times 10^{-5}$
	3) $52{,}000{,}000 = 5.2 \times 10^7$	4) $21{,}000 = 2.1 \times 10^4$
	5) $3 \times 10^{-1} = 0.3$	6) $5 \times 10^{-2} = 0.05$
	7) $1.2 \times 10^3 = 1{,}200$	8) $2 \times 10^{-4} = 0.0002$

Name:	**Date:** ....

Topic	Radicals
Notes	✓ If n is a positive integer and x is a real number, then: $\sqrt[n]{x} = x^{\frac{1}{n}}$, $\sqrt[n]{xy} = x^{\frac{1}{n}} \times y^{\frac{1}{n}}$, $\sqrt[n]{\frac{x}{y}} = \frac{x^{\frac{1}{n}}}{y^{\frac{1}{n}}}$, and $\sqrt[n]{x} \times \sqrt[n]{y} = \sqrt[n]{xy}$ ✓ A square root of x is a number r whose square is: $r^2 = x$ (r is a square root of x. ✓ To add and subtract radicals, we need to have the same values under the radical. For example: $\sqrt{3} + \sqrt{3} = 2\sqrt{3}$, $3\sqrt{5} - \sqrt{5} = 2\sqrt{5}$
Example	***Evaluate.*** $\sqrt{32} + \sqrt{8} =$ **Solution:** Since we do not have the same values under the radical, we cannot add these two radicals. But we can simplify each radical. $\sqrt{32} = \sqrt{16} \times \sqrt{2} = 4\sqrt{2}$ and $\sqrt{8} = \sqrt{4} \times \sqrt{2} = 2\sqrt{2}$ Now, we have the same values under the radical. Then: $$\sqrt{32} + \sqrt{8} = 4\sqrt{2} + 2\sqrt{2} = 6\sqrt{2}$$
Your Turn!	1) $\sqrt{9} \times \sqrt{9} =$ 2) $\sqrt{8} \times \sqrt{2} =$ 3) $\sqrt{3} \times \sqrt{27} =$ 4) $\sqrt{32} \div \sqrt{2} =$ 5) $\sqrt{2} + \sqrt{8} =$ 6) $\sqrt{27} - \sqrt{3} =$ 7) $4\sqrt{5} - 2\sqrt{5} =$ 8) $3\sqrt{3} \times 2\sqrt{3} =$

Name:	Date: ....

Topic	Radicals - Answers
Notes	✓ If n is a positive integer and x is a real number, then: $\sqrt[n]{x} = x^{\frac{1}{n}}$, $\sqrt[n]{xy} = x^{\frac{1}{n}} \times y^{\frac{1}{n}}$, $\sqrt[n]{\frac{x}{y}} = \frac{x^{\frac{1}{n}}}{y^{\frac{1}{n}}}$, and $\sqrt[n]{x} \times \sqrt[n]{y} = \sqrt[n]{xy}$ ✓ A square root of x is a number r whose square is: $r^2 = x$ (r is a square root of x. ✓ To add and subtract radicals, we need to have the same values under the radical. For example: $\sqrt{3} + \sqrt{3} = 2\sqrt{3}$, $3\sqrt{5} - \sqrt{5} = 2\sqrt{5}$
Example	*Evaluate.* $\sqrt{32} + \sqrt{8} =$ **Solution:** Since we do not have the same values under the radical, we cannot add these two radicals. But we can simplify each radical. $\sqrt{32} = \sqrt{16} \times \sqrt{2} = 4\sqrt{2}$ and $\sqrt{8} = \sqrt{4} \times \sqrt{2} = 2\sqrt{2}$ Now, we have the same values under the radical. Then: $$\sqrt{32} + \sqrt{8} = 4\sqrt{2} + 2\sqrt{2} = 6\sqrt{2}$$
Your Turn!	1) $\sqrt{9} \times \sqrt{9} = 9$ 2) $\sqrt{8} \times \sqrt{2} = 4$ 3) $\sqrt{3} \times \sqrt{27} = 9$ 4) $\sqrt{32} \div \sqrt{2} = 4$ 5) $\sqrt{2} + \sqrt{8} = 3\sqrt{2}$ 6) $\sqrt{27} - \sqrt{3} = 2\sqrt{3}$ 7) $4\sqrt{5} - 2\sqrt{5} = 2\sqrt{5}$ 8) $3\sqrt{3} \times 2\sqrt{3} = 18$

Name:	**Date:** ....

Topic	**Simplifying Polynomials**
Notes	✓ Find "like" terms. (they have same variables with same power). ✓ Use "FOIL". (First–Out–In–Last) for binomials: $$(x + a)(x + b) = x^2 + (b + a)x + ab$$ ✓ Add or Subtract "like" terms using order of operation.
Example	***Simplify this expression.*** $(x + 3)(x - 8) =$ **Solution:** First apply FOIL method: $(a + b)(c + d) = ac + ad + bc + bd$ $(x + 3)(x - 8) = x^2 - 8x + 3x - 24$ Now combine like terms: $x^2 - 8x + 3x - 24 = x^2 - 5x - 24$

Your Turn!	1) $-(2x - 4) =$ _____	2) $2(2x + 6) =$ _____
	3) $3x(3x - 4) =$ _____	4) $5x(2x + 8) =$ _____
	5) $-2x(5x + 6) + 5x =$ _____	6) $-4x(8x - 3) - x^2 =$ _____
	7) $(x + 4)(x + 5) =$ _____	8) $(x + 2)(x + 8) =$ _____
	9) $-4x^2 + 10x^3 + 5x^2 =$ _____	10) $-3x^5 + 10x^4 + 5x^5 =$ _____

Name:	Date: ....

Topic	**Simplifying Polynomials - Answers**	
Notes	✓ Find "like" terms. (they have same variables with same power). ✓ Use "FOIL". (First–Out–In–Last) for binomials: $$(x + a)(x + b) = x^2 + (b + a)x + ab$$ ✓ Add or Subtract "like" terms using order of operation.	
Example	**_Simplify this expression_**. $(x + 3)(x - 8) =$ **Solution:** First apply FOIL method: $(a + b)(c + d) = ac + ad + bc + bd$ $(x + 3)(x - 8) = x^2 - 8x + 3x - 24$ Now combine like terms: $x^2 - 8x + 3x - 24 = x^2 - 5x - 24$	
Your Turn!	1) $-(2x - 4) =$ $-2x + 4$	2) $2(2x + 6) =$ $4x + 12$
	3) $3x(3x - 4) =$ $9x^2 - 12x$	4) $5x(2x + 8) =$ $10x^2 + 40x$
	5) $-2x(5x + 6) + 5x =$ $-10x^2 - 7x$	6) $-4x(8x - 3) - x^2 =$ $-33x^2 + 12x$
	7) $(x + 4)(x + 5) =$ $x^2 + 9x + 20$	8) $(x + 2)(x + 8) =$ $x^2 + 10x + 16$
	9) $-4x^2 + 10x^3 + 5x^2 =$ $10x^3 + x^2$	10) $-3x^5 + 10x^4 + 5x^5 =$ $2x^5 + 10x^4$

Name:	Date: ....

Topic	**Adding and Subtracting Polynomials**	
Notes	✓ Adding polynomials is just a matter of combining like terms, with some order of operations considerations thrown in. ✓ Be careful with the minus signs, and don't confuse addition and multiplication!	
Example	**Simplify the expressions.** $(3x^2 - 4x^3) - (5x^3 - 8x^2) =$ **Solution:** First use Distributive Property: $-(5x^3 - 8x^2) = -5x^3 + 8x^2$ → $(3x^2 - 4x^3) - (5x^3 - 8x^2) = 3x^2 - 4x^3 - 5x^3 + 8x^2$ Now combine like terms: $3x^2 - 4x^3 - 5x^3 + 8x^2 = -9x^3 + 11x^2$	
Your Turn!	1) $(x^2 - x) + (4x^2 - 5) =$ _____	2) $(2x^3 + x) - (x^3 + 2) =$ _____
	3) $(x^2 - 5x) + (6x^2 - 5) =$ _____	4) $(8x^2 - 2) - (3x^2 + 7) =$ _____
	5) $(3x^2 + 2) - (2 - 4x^2) =$ _____	6) $(x^3 + x^2) - (x^3 - 10) =$ _____
	7) $(3x^3 - 2x) - (x - x^3) =$ _____	8) $(x - 5x^4) - (2x^4 + 3x) =$ _____
	9) $(6x^3 + 5) - (4 - 5x^3) =$ _____	10) $(2x^2 + 5x^3) - (6x^3 + 7) =$ _____

Name:	Date: ....

Topic	**Adding and Subtracting Polynomials - Answers**
Notes	✓ Adding polynomials is just a matter of combining like terms, with some order of operations considerations thrown in. ✓ Be careful with the minus signs, and don't confuse addition and multiplication!
Example	**Simplify the expressions.** $(3x^2 - 4x^3) - (5x^3 - 8x^2) =$ **Solution:** First use Distributive Property: $-(5x^3 - 8x^2) = -5x^3 + 8x^2$ $\rightarrow (3x^2 - 4x^3) - (5x^3 - 8x^2) = 3x^2 - 4x^3 - 5x^3 + 8x^2$ Now combine like terms: $3x^2 - 4x^3 - 5x^3 + 8x^2 = -9x^3 + 11x^2$

Your Turn!	1) $(x^2 - x) + (4x^2 - 5) =$ $5x^2 - x - 5$	2) $(2x^3 + x) - (x^3 + 2) =$ $x^3 + x - 2$
	3) $(x^2 - 5x) + (6x^2 - 5) =$ $7x^2 - 5x - 5$	4) $(8x^2 - 2) - (3x^2 + 7) =$ $5x^2 - 9$
	5) $(3x^2 + 2) - (2 - 4x^2) =$ $7x^2$	6) $(x^3 + x^2) - (x^3 - 10) =$ $x^2 + 10$
	7) $(3x^3 - 2x) - (x - x^3) =$ $4x^3 - 3x$	8) $(x - 5x^4) - (2x^4 + 3x) =$ $7x^4 - 2x$
	9) $(6x^3 + 5) - (4 - 5x^3) =$ $11x^3 + 1$	10) $(2x^2 + 5x^3) - (6x^3 + 7) =$ $-x^3 + 2x^2 - 7$

Name: .... **Date:** ....

Topic	**Multiplying Binomials**
Notes	✓ A binomial is a polynomial that is the sum or the difference of two terms, each of which is a monomial. ✓ To multiply two binomials, use "FOIL" method. (First–Out–In–Last) $(x + a)(x + b) = x \times x + x \times b + a \times x + a \times b = x^2 + bx + ax + ab$
Example	**Multiply.** $(x - 4)(x + 9) =$ **Solution:** Use "FOIL". (First–Out–In–Last): $(x - 4)(x + 9) = x^2 + 9x - 4x - 36$ Then simplify: $x^2 + 9x - 4x - 36 = x^2 + 5x - 36$
Your Turn!	1) $(x + 2)(x + 2) =$ _____ $\qquad$ 2) $(x + 3)(x + 2) =$ _____ 3) $(x - 3)(x + 4) =$ _____ $\qquad$ 4) $(x - 2)(x - 4) =$ _____ 5) $(x + 3)(x + 4) =$ _____ $\qquad$ 6) $(x + 5)(x + 4) =$ _____ 7) $(x - 6)(x - 5) =$ _____ $\qquad$ 8) $(x - 5)(x - 5) =$ _____ 9) $(x + 6)(x - 8) =$ _____ $\qquad$ 10) $(x - 9)(x + 7) =$ _____

Name:	Date: ....

Topic	**Multiplying Binomials - Answers**	
Notes	✓A binomial is a polynomial that is the sum or the difference of two terms, each of which is a monomial. ✓To multiply two binomials, use "FOIL" method. (First–Out–In–Last) $$(x + a)(x + b) = x \times x + x \times b + a \times x + a \times b = x^2 + bx + ax + ab$$	
Example	**Multiply.** $(x - 4)(x + 9) =$ **Solution:** Use "FOIL". (First–Out–In–Last): $(x - 4)(x + 9) = x^2 + 9x - 4x - 36$ Then simplify: $x^2 + 9x - 4x - 36 = x^2 + 5x - 36$	
Your Turn!	1) $(x + 2)(x + 2) =$ $x^2 + 4x + 4$	2) $(x + 3)(x + 2) =$ $x^2 + 5x + 6$
	3) $(x - 3)(x + 4) =$ $x^2 + x - 12$	4) $(x - 2)(x - 4) =$ $x^2 - 6x + 8$
	5) $(x + 3)(x + 4) =$ $x^2 + 7x + 12$	6) $(x + 5)(x + 4) =$ $x^2 + 9x + 20$
	7) $(x - 6)(x - 5) =$ $x^2 - 11x + 30$	8) $(x - 5)(x - 5) =$ $x^2 - 10x + 25$
	9) $(x + 6)(x - 8) =$ $x^2 - 2x - 48$	10) $(x - 9)(x + 7) =$ $x^2 - 2x - 63$

Name:	Date: ....

Topic	**Multiplying and Dividing Monomials**
Notes	✓ When you divide or multiply two monomials you need to divide or multiply their coefficients and then divide or multiply their variables. ✓ In case of exponents with the same base, you need to subtract their powers. ✓ Exponent's rules: $$x^a \times x^b = x^{a+b}, \qquad \frac{x^a}{x^b} = x^{a-b}$$ $$\frac{1}{x^b} = x^{-b}, \quad (x^a)^b = x^{a \times b}$$ $$(xy)^a = x^a \times y^a$$
Example	***Divide expressions.*** $\frac{-18x^5y^6}{2xy^2} =$ **Solution:** Use exponents' division rule: $\frac{x^a}{x^b} = x^{a-b}, \frac{x^5}{x} = x^{5-1} = x^4$ and $\frac{y^6}{y^2} = y^4$ Then: $\frac{-18x^5y^6}{2xy^2} = -9x^4y^4$
Your Turn!	1) $(x^8y)(xy^2) =$ _____ 3) $(x^7y^4)(2x^5y^2) =$ _____ 5) $(-6x^8y^7)(4x^6y^9) =$ _____ 7) $\frac{30x^8y^9}{6x^5y^4} =$ _____	2) $(x^4y^3)(x^2y^3) =$ _____ 4) $(3x^5y^4)(4x^6y^3) =$ _____ 6) $(-2x^9y^3)(9x^7y^8) =$ _____ 8) $\frac{-42x^{12}y^{16}}{7x^8y^9} =$ _____

| Name: .... | Date: .... |

Topic	**Multiplying and Dividing Monomials - Answers**
Notes	✓ When you divide or multiply two monomials you need to divide or multiply their coefficients and then divide or multiply their variables. ✓ In case of exponents with the same base, you need to subtract their powers. ✓ Exponent's rules: $$x^a \times x^b = x^{a+b}, \quad \frac{x^a}{x^b} = x^{a-b}$$ $$\frac{1}{x^b} = x^{-b}, \quad (x^a)^b = x^{a \times b}$$ $$(xy)^a = x^a \times y^a$$
Example	**Divide expressions.** $\frac{-18x^5y^6}{2xy^2} =$ **Solution:** Use exponents' division rule: $\frac{x^a}{x^b} = x^{a-b}, \frac{x^5}{x} = x^{5-1} = x^4$ and $\frac{y^6}{y^2} = y^4$ Then: $\frac{-18x^5y^6}{2xy^2} = -9x^4y^4$
Your Turn!	1) $(x^8y)(xy^2) =$ x^9y^3 2) $(x^4y^3)(x^2y^3) =$ x^6y^6 3) $(x^7y^4)(2x^5y^2) =$ $2x^{12}y^6$ 4) $(3x^5y^4)(4x^6y^3) =$ $12x^{11}y^7$ 5) $(-6x^8y^7)(4x^6y^9) =$ $-24x^{14}y^{16}$ 6) $(-2x^9y^3)(9x^7y^8) =$ $-18x^{16}y^{11}$ 7) $\frac{30x^8y^9}{6x^5y^4} =$ $5x^3y^5$ 8) $\frac{-42x^{12}y^{16}}{7x^8y^9} =$ $-6x^4y^7$

Name:	Date: ....

Topic	**Multiplying a Polynomial and a Monomial**
Notes	✓ When multiplying monomials, use the product rule for exponents. $x^a \times x^b = x^{a+b}$ ✓ When multiplying a monomial by a polynomial, use the distributive property. $$a \times (b + c) = a \times b + a \times c = ab + ac$$ $$a \times (b - c) = a \times b - a \times c = ab - ac$$
Example	***Multiply expressions.*** $4x(5x - 8) =$ **Solution:** Use Distributive Property: $4x(5x - 8) = 4x \times 5x - 4x \times (8) =$ Now, simplify: $4x \times 5x - 4x \times (8) = 20x^2 - 32x$

Your Turn!	1) $3x(2x + y) =$ _____	2) $x(x - 3y) =$ _____
	3) $-x(5x - 3y) =$ _____	4) $4x(x + 5y) =$ _____
	5) $-x(5x + 8y) =$ _____	6) $2x(6x - 7y) =$ _____
	7) $-3x(x^3 + 4y^2 - 6x) =$ _____	8) $7x(x^2 - 5y^2 + 4) =$ _____

| Name: .... | Date: .... |

Topic	**Multiplying a Polynomial and a Monomial - Answers**
Notes	✓ When multiplying monomials, use the product rule for exponents. $x^a \times x^b = x^{a+b}$ ✓ When multiplying a monomial by a polynomial, use the distributive property. $$a \times (b + c) = a \times b + a \times c = ab + ac$$ $$a \times (b - c) = a \times b - a \times c = ab - ac$$
Example	*Multiply expressions.* $4x(5x - 8) =$ **Solution:** Use Distributive Property: $4x(5x - 8) = 4x \times 5x - 4x \times (8) =$ Now, simplify: $4x \times 5x - 4x \times (8) = 20x^2 - 32x$

Your Turn!	1) $3x(2x + y) =$ $6x^2 + 3xy$	2) $x(x - 3y) =$ $x^2 - 3xy$
	3) $-x(5x - 3y) =$ $-5x^2 + 3xy$	4) $4x(x + 5y) =$ $4x^2 + 20xy$
	5) $-x(5x + 8y) =$ $-5x^2 - 8xy$	6) $2x(6x - 7y) =$ $12x^2 - 14xy$
	7) $-3x(x^3 + 4y^2 - 6x) =$ $-3x^4 - 12xy^2 + 18x^2$	8) $7x(x^2 - 5y^2 + 4) =$ $7x^3 - 35xy^2 + 28x$

| Name: .... | Date: .... |

Topic	**Multiplying Monomials**
Notes	✓ A monomial is a polynomial with just one term: Examples: $5x$ or $7x^2yz^8$. ✓ When you multiply monomials, first multiply the coefficients (a number placed before and multiplying the variable) and then multiply the variables using multiplication property of exponents. $x^a \times x^b = x^{a+b}$
Example	**Multiply.** $(-3xy^4z^5) \times (2x^2y^5z^3) =$ **Solution:** Multiply coefficients and find same variables and use multiplication property of exponents: $x^a \times x^b = x^{a+b}$ $-3 \times 2 = -6$, $x \times x^2 = x^{1+2} = x^3$, $y^4 \times y^5 = y^{4+5} = y^9$, and $z^2 \times z^5 = z^{2+5} = z^7$ Then: $(-3xy^4z^5) \times (2x^2y^5z^3) = -6x^3y^9z^7$
Your Turn!	1) $2x^2 \times 4x^6 =$ _____ 2) $5x^7 \times 6x^4 =$ _____ 3) $-2x^2y^4 \times 6x^3y^2 =$ _____ 4) $-5x^5y \times 3x^3y^4 =$ _____ 5) $8x^7y^5 \times 5x^6y^3 =$ _____ 6) $-6x^7y^5 \times (-3x^9y^8) =$ _____ 7) $12x^8y^8z^4 \times 3x^4y^3z =$ _____ 8) $-8x^9y^7z^{11} \times 7x^6y^7z^5 =$ _____

Name:	Date: ....

Topic	**Multiplying Monomials**	
Notes	✓ A monomial is a polynomial with just one term: Examples: $5x$ or $7x^2yz^8$. ✓ When you multiply monomials, first multiply the coefficients (a number placed before and multiplying the variable) and then multiply the variables using multiplication property of exponents. $x^a \times x^b = x^{a+b}$	
Example	**Multiply.** $(-3xy^4z^5) \times (2x^2y^5z^3) =$ **Solution:** Multiply coefficients and find same variables and use multiplication property of exponents: $x^a \times x^b = x^{a+b}$ $-3 \times 2 = -6$, $x \times x^2 = x^{1+2} = x^3$, $y^4 \times y^5 = y^{4+5} = y^9$, and $z^2 \times z^5 = z^{2+5} = z^7$ Then: $(-3xy^4z^5) \times (2x^2y^5z^3) = -6x^3y^9z^7$	
Your Turn!	1) $2x^2 \times 4x^6 =$ $8x^8$	2) $5x^7 \times 6x^4 =$ $30x^{11}$
	3) $-2x^2y^4 \times 6x^3y^2 =$ $-12x^5y^6$	4) $-5x^5y \times 3x^3y^4 =$ $-15x^8y^5$
	5) $8x^7y^5 \times 5x^6y^3 =$ $40x^{13}y^8$	6) $-6x^7y^5 \times (-3x^9y^8) =$ $18x^{16}y^{13}$
	7) $12x^8y^8z^4 \times 3x^4y^3z =$ $36x^{12}y^{11}z^5$	8) $-8x^9y^7z^{11} \times 7x^6y^7z^5 =$ $-56x^{15}y^{14}z^{16}$

| Name: .... | Date: .... |

Topic	**Factoring Trinomials**
Notes	To factor trinomial, use of the following methods: ✓ "FOIL": $(x + a)(x + b) = x^2 + (b + a)x + ab$ ✓ "Difference of Squares": $$a^2 - b^2 = (a + b)(a - b)$$ $$a^2 + 2ab + b^2 = (a + b)(a + b)$$ $$a^2 - 2ab + b^2 = (a - b)(a - b)$$ ✓ "Reverse FOIL": $x^2 + (b + a)x + ab = (x + a)(x + b)$
Example	***Factor this trinomial.*** $x^2 + 12x + 32 =$ **Solution:** Break the expression into groups: $(x^2 + 4x) + (8x + 32)$ Now factor out x from $x^2 + 4x : x(x + 4)$, and factor out 8 from $8x + 32$: $8(x + 4)$ Then: $(x^2 + 4x) + (8x + 32) = x(x + 4) + 8(x + 4)$ Now factor out like term: $(x + 4) \rightarrow (x + 4)(x + 8)$
Your Turn!	1) $x^2 + 6x + 9 =$ _____ 2) $x^2 + 5x + 6 =$ _____

1) $x^2 + 6x + 9 =$ _____	2) $x^2 + 5x + 6 =$ _____
3) $x^2 + x + 12 =$ _____	4) $x^2 - 6x + 8 =$ _____
5) $x^2 + 7x + 12 =$ _____	6) $x^2 + 12x + 32 =$ _____
7) $x^2 - 11x + 30 =$ _____	8) $x^2 - 14x + 45 =$ _____

Name: ....

Date: ....

Topic	**Factoring Trinomials - Answers**
Notes	To factor trinomial, use of the following methods: ✓ "FOIL": $(x + a)(x + b) = x^2 + (b + a)x + ab$ ✓ "Difference of Squares": $$a^2 - b^2 = (a + b)(a - b)$$ $$a^2 + 2ab + b^2 = (a + b)(a + b)$$ $$a^2 - 2ab + b^2 = (a - b)(a - b)$$ ✓ "Reverse FOIL": $x^2 + (b + a)x + ab = (x + a)(x + b)$
Example	**Factor this trinomial.** $x^2 + 12x + 32 =$ **Solution:** Break the expression into groups: $(x^2 + 4x) + (8x + 32)$ Now factor out x from $x^2 + 4x$: $x(x + 4)$, and factor out 8 from $8x + 32$: $8(x + 4)$ Then: $(x^2 + 4x) + (8x + 32) = x(x + 4) + 8(x + 4)$ Now factor out like term: $(x + 4) \rightarrow (x + 4)(x + 8)$

Your Turn!

1) $x^2 + 6x + 9 =$ $(x + 3)(x + 3)$	2) $x^2 + 5x + 6 =$ $(x + 3)(x + 2)$
3) $x^2 + x + 12 =$ $(x - 3)(x + 4)$	4) $x^2 - 6x + 8 =$ $(x - 2)(x - 4)$
5) $x^2 + 7x + 12 =$ $(x + 3)(x + 4)$	6) $x^2 + 12x + 32 =$ $(x + 8)(x + 4)$
7) $x^2 - 11x + 30 =$ $(x - 6)(x - 5)$	8) $x^2 - 14x + 45 =$ $(x - 9)(x - 5)$

| Name: .... | Date: .... |

Topic	The Pythagorean Theorem
Notes	✓ In any right triangle: $a^2 + b^2 = c^2$
Example	Right triangle ABC (not shown) has two legs of lengths 18 cm (AB) and 24 cm (AC). What is the length of the third side (BC)? **Solution:** Use Pythagorean Theorem: $a^2 + b^2 = c^2$ Then: $a^2 + b^2 = c^2 \rightarrow 18^2 + 24^2 = c^2 \rightarrow 324 + 576 = c^2$ $c^2 = 900 \rightarrow c = \sqrt{900} = 30\ cm$
Your Turn!	1) _____ 2) _____ 3) _____ 4) _____

1) _____

15   ?

8

2) _____

16   34

?

3) _____

13

5

?

4) _____

15

?   12

Name: .... **Date:** ....

Topic	**The Pythagorean Theorem - Answers**
Notes	✓ In any right triangle: $a^2 + b^2 = c^2$
Example	Right triangle ABC (not shown) has two legs of lengths 18 cm (AB) and 24 cm (AC). What is the length of the third side (BC)? **Solution:** Use Pythagorean Theorem: $a^2 + b^2 = c^2$ Then: $a^2 + b^2 = c^2 \rightarrow 18^2 + 24^2 = c^2 \rightarrow 324 + 576 = c^2$ $c^2 = 900 \rightarrow c = \sqrt{900} = 30\ cm$
Your Turn!	1) 17 2) 30 15, ?, 8 34, 16, ? 3) 12 4) 9 13, 5, ? 15, ?, 12

Name:	Date: ....

Topic	Triangles
Notes	✓ In any triangle the sum of all angles is 180 degrees. ✓ Area of a triangle = $\frac{1}{2}$ $(base \times height)$ *h* *b*
Example	*What is the area of the following triangle?* 6 16 **Solution:** Use the area formula: Area $= \frac{1}{2}$ $(base \times height)$ $base = 16$ and $height = 6$ Area $= \frac{1}{2}(16 \times 6) = \frac{96}{2} = 48$
Your Turn!	5) _____ 24 10 6) _____ 18 28 7) _____ 20 30 8) _____ 32 46

| Name: .... | Date: .... |

Topic	**Triangles - Answers**
Notes	✓ In any triangle the sum of all angles is 180 degrees. ✓ Area of a triangle = $\frac{1}{2}$ (*base* × *height*) h b
Example	*What is the area of the following triangle?* 6 16 **Solution:** Use the area formula: Area = $\frac{1}{2}$ (*base* × *height*) *base* = 16 and *height* = 6 Area = $\frac{1}{2}(16 \times 6) = \frac{96}{2} = 48$

Your Turn!

5) 120

24
10

6) 252

18
28

7) 300

20
30

8) 736

32
46

Name:	Date: ....

Topic	Polygons

Notes	Perimeter of a square $= 4 \times side = 4s$ Perimeter of a rectangle $= 2(width + length)$ Perimeter of trapezoid $= a + b + c + d$ Perimeter of a regular hexagon $= 6a$ Perimeter of a parallelogram $= 2(l + w)$

Example	**Find the perimeter of following regular hexagon.** **Solution:** Since the hexagon is regular, all sides are equal. Then: Perimeter of Hexagon $= 6 \times (one\ side)$ Perimeter of Hexagon $= 6 \times (one\ side) = 6 \times 9 = 54\ m$

Your Turn!

9) (rectangle) _____

9 in

15 in

10) _____

8 m

10 m   10 m

14 m

11)   (regular hexagon) 5 m _____

12)   (parallelogram)_____

10 in

16 in

Name: ....

Date: ....

Topic	Polygons - Answers
Notes	Perimeter of a square $= 4 \times side = 4s$ Perimeter of a rectangle $= 2(width + length)$ Perimeter of trapezoid $= a + b + c + d$ Perimeter of a regular hexagon $= 6a$ Perimeter of a parallelogram $= 2(l + w)$
Example	**Find the perimeter of following regular hexagon.** **Solution:** Since the hexagon is regular, all sides are equal. Then: Perimeter of Hexagon $= 6 \times (one\ side)$ Perimeter of Hexagon $= 6 \times (one\ side) = 6 \times 9 = 54\ m$
Your Turn!	9) *(rectangle)* 48 in 9 in, 15 in 11) *(regular hexagon)* 30 m 5 m 10) 42 m 8 m, 10 m, 10 m, 14 m 12) *(parallelogram)* 52 in 10 in, 16 in

| Name: .... | Date: .... |

Topic	Circles
Notes	✓ In a circle, variable r is usually used for the radius and d for diameter and π is about 3.14. ✓ *Area of a circle* $= \pi r^2$ ✓ *Circumference of a circle* $= 2\pi r$ r
Example	**Find the area of the circle.** **Solution:** Use area formula: $Area = \pi r^2$ $r = 2\ in \rightarrow Area = \pi(2)^2 = 4\pi,\ \pi = 3.14$ **Then:** $Area = 4 \times 3.14 = 12.56\ in^2$ $2\ in$
Your Turn!	**Find the area of each circle.** $(\pi = 3.14)$ 1) _____ 6 cm 2) _____ 10 in **Find the Circumference of each circle.** $(\pi = 3.14)$ 3) _____ 8 cm 4) _____ 6 m

Name:	Date: ....

Topic	**Circles - Answers**
Notes	✓ In a circle, variable r is usually used for the radius and d for diameter and π is about 3.14. ✓ $Area\ of\ a\ circle = \pi r^2$ ✓ $Circumference\ of\ a\ circle = 2\pi r$

Find the area of the circle.

Example

    Solution:
Use area formula: $Area = \pi r^2$
$r = 2\ in \rightarrow Area = \pi(2)^2 = 4\pi, \pi = 3.14$
Then: $Area = 4 \times 3.14 = 12.56\ in^2$

Find the area of each circle. ($\pi = 3.14$)

1) $113.04\ cm^2$

2) $314\ in^2$

Find the Circumference of each circle. ($\pi = 3.14$)

Your Turn!

3) $50.24\ cm$

4) $37.68\ m$

Name:	**Date:** ....

Topic	**Cubes**
Notes	✓ A cube is a three-dimensional solid object bounded by six square sides. ✓ Volume is the measure of the amount of space inside of a solid figure, like a cube, ball, cylinder or pyramid. ✓ Volume of a cube $= (one\ side)^3$ ✓ surface area of cube $= 6 \times (one\ side)^2$
Example	**Find the volume and surface area of the following cube.** 15 cm **Solution:** Use volume formula: $volume = (one\ side)^3$ Then: $volume = (one\ side)^3 = (15)^3 = 3,375\ cm^3$ Use surface area formula: $surface\ area\ of\ cube: 6(one\ side)^2 = 6(15)^2 = 6(225) = 1,350\ cm^2$
Your Turn!	**Find the volume of each cube.** 1) _____ 11 in 2) _____ 13 ft 3) _____ 14 cm 4) _____ 30 m

Name:	Date: ....

Topic	**Cubes - Answers**
Notes	✓ A cube is a three-dimensional solid object bounded by six square sides. ✓ Volume is the measure of the amount of space inside of a solid figure, like a cube, ball, cylinder or pyramid. ✓ Volume of a cube $= (one\ side)^3$ ✓ surface area of cube $= 6 \times (one\ side)^2$
Example	*Find the volume and surface area of the following cube.* 15 cm **Solution:** Use volume formula: $volume = (one\ side)^3$ Then: $volume = (one\ side)^3 = (15)^3 = 3,375\ cm^3$ Use surface area formula: $surface\ area\ of\ cube: 6(one\ side)^2 = 6(15)^2 = 6(225) = 1,350\ cm^2$

Find the volume of each cube.

1) $1,331\ in^3$ 11 in	2) $2,197\ ft^3$ 13 ft
3) $2,744\ cm^3$ 14 cm	4) $27,000\ m^3$ 30 m

Your Turn!

Name:	Date: ....

Topic	Trapezoids
Notes	✓ A quadrilateral with at least one pair of parallel sides is a trapezoid. ✓ Area of a trapezoid = $\frac{1}{2}h(b_1 + b_2)$
Example	**Calculate the area of the trapezoid.** **Solution:** Use area formula: $A = \frac{1}{2}h(b_1 + b_2)$ $b_1 = 8\ cm$, $b_2 = 12\ cm$ and $h = 14\ cm$ Then: $A = \frac{1}{2}(14)(12 + 8) = 7(20) = 140\ cm^2$
Your Turn!	1) _____ 5 cm 4 cm 9 cm 2) _____ 8 m 10 m 12 m 3) _____ 7 ft 6 ft 15 ft 4) _____ 10 cm 8 cm 14 cm

Name: ....   **Date:** ....

Topic	Trapezoids - Answers
Notes	✓ A quadrilateral with at least one pair of parallel sides is a trapezoid. ✓ Area of a trapezoid = $\frac{1}{2}h(b_1 + b_2)$
Example	**Calculate the area of the trapezoid.** **Solution:** Use area formula: $A = \frac{1}{2}h(b_1 + b_2)$ $b_1 = 8\ cm$, $b_2 = 12\ cm$ and $h = 14\ cm$ Then: $A = \frac{1}{2}(14)(12 + 8) = 7(20) = 140\ cm^2$
Your Turn!	1) $28\ cm^2$ 2) $100\ m^2$ 3) $66\ ft^2$ 4) $96\ cm^2$

Name:	Date: ....

Topic	**Rectangular Prisms**
Notes	✓ A solid 3-dimensional object which has six rectangular faces. ✓ Volume of a Rectangular prism = $Length \times Width \times Height$ $Volume = l \times w \times h$ $Surface\ area = 2(wh + lw + lh)$
Example	**Find the volume and surface area of rectangular prism.** **Solution:** Use volume formula: $Volume = l \times w \times h$ Then: $Volume = 4 \times 2 \times 6 = 48\ m^3$ Use surface area formula: $Surface\ area = 2(wh + lw + lh)$ Then: $Surface\ area = 2\big((2 \times 6) + (4 \times 2) + (4 \times 6)\big)$ $= 2(12 + 8 + 24) = 2(44) = 88\ m^2$
Your Turn!	**Find the surface area of each Rectangular Prism.** 1) _____ 6 ft, 10 ft, 4 ft 2) _____ 8 cm, 16 cm, 6 cm 3) _____ 12 m, 18 m, 10 m 4) _____ 20 in, 15 in, 12 in

| Name: .... | Date: .... |

Topic	**Rectangular Prisms - Answers**
Notes	✓ A solid 3-dimensional object which has six rectangular faces. ✓ Volume of a Rectangular prism = **Length × Width × Height** $Volume = l \times w \times h$ $Surface\ area = 2(wh + lw + lh)$

Example

Find the volume and surface area of rectangular prism.
Solution:
Use volume formula: $Volume = l \times w \times h$

Then: $Volume = 4 \times 2 \times 6 = 48\ m^3$

Use surface area formula: $Surface\ area = 2(wh + lw + lh)$

Then: $Surface\ area = 2\big((2 \times 6) + (4 \times 2) + (4 \times 6)\big)$

$= 2(12 + 8 + 24) = 2(44) = 88\ m^2$

Your Turn!

Find the surface area of each Rectangular Prism.

1) $248\ ft^2$

2) $544\ cm^2$

3) $1,032\ m^2$

4) $1,440\ in^2$

Name: .... **Date:** ....

Topic	Cylinder

Notes	✓ A cylinder is a solid geometric figure with straight parallel sides and a circular or oval cross section. ✓ *Volume of Cylinder Formula* $= \pi(radius)^2 \times height$ $\pi = 3.14$ ✓ *Surface area of a cylinder* $= 2\pi r^2 + 2\pi rh$

height

radius

Example	**Find the volume and Surface area of the follow Cylinder.** Solution: Use volume formula: $Volume = \pi(radius)^2 \times height$ Then: $Volume = \pi(3)^2 \times 12 = 9\pi \times 12 = 108\pi$ $\pi = 3.14$ **then:** $Volume = 108\pi = 339.12\ cm^3$ Use surface area formula: $Surface\ area = 2\pi r^2 + 2\pi rh$ **Then:** $2\pi(3)^2 + 2\pi(3)(12) = 2\pi(9) + 2\pi(36) = 18\pi + 72\pi = 90\pi$ $\pi = 3.14$ **Then:** $Surface\ area = 90 \times 3.14 = 282.6\ cm^2$

12 cm 3 cm

Your Turn!	**Find the volume of each Cylinder.** ($\pi = 3.14$) 1) _____ 10 in 2 in 2) _____ 14 m 5 m **Find the Surface area of each Cylinder.** ($\pi = 3.14$) 3) _____ 15 ft 9 ft 4) _____ 20 cm 12 cm

Name:	Date: ....

Topic	**Cylinder - Answers**
Notes	✓ A cylinder is a solid geometric figure with straight parallel sides and a circular or oval cross section. ✓ *Volume of Cylinder Formula* $= \pi(radius)^2 \times height$ $\pi = 3.14$ ✓ *Surface area of a cylinder* $= 2\pi r^2 + 2\pi rh$

Example	**Find the volume and Surface area of the follow Cylinder.** Solution: Use volume formula: $Volume = \pi(radius)^2 \times height$ Then: $Volume = \pi(3)^2 \times 12 = 9\pi \times 12 = 108\pi$ $\pi = 3.14$ **then:** $Volume = 108\pi = 339.12 \ cm^3$ Use surface area formula: $Surface\ area = 2\pi r^2 + 2\pi rh$ **Then:** $2\pi(3)^2 + 2\pi(3)(12) = 2\pi(9) + 2\pi(36) = 18\pi + 72\pi = 90\pi$ $\pi = 3.14$ **Then:** $Surface\ area = 90 \times 3.14 = 282.6 \ cm^2$ $12\ cm$ $3\ cm$

Your Turn!	**Find the volume of each Cylinder.** ($\pi = 3.14$)

1) $125.6 \ in^3$ $10\ in$ $2\ in$	2) $1{,}099 \ m^3$ $14\ m$ $5\ m$
Find the Surface area of each Cylinder. ($\pi = 3.14$)	
3) $1{,}356.48 \ ft^2$ $15\ ft$ $9\ ft$	4) $2{,}411.52 \ cm^2$ $20\ cm$ $12\ cm$

Name:	Date: ....

Topic	**Mean, Median, Mode, and Range of the Given Data**
Notes	✓ Mean: $\dfrac{sum\ of\ the\ data}{total\ number\ of\ data\ entires}$ ✓ Mode: value in the list that appears most often. ✓ Median: is the middle number of a group of numbers that have been arranged in order by size. ✓ Range: the difference of largest value and smallest value in the list.
Example	*Find the mode and median of these numbers?* $16, 10, 6, 3, 1, 16, 2, 4$ **Solution:** Mode: value in the list that appears most often. Number 16 is the value in the list that appears most often (there are two number 16). To find median, write the numbers in order: $1, 2, 3, 4, 6, 10, 16, 16$ Number 4 and 6 are in the middle. Find their average: $\dfrac{4+6}{2} = \dfrac{10}{2} = 5$ The median is 5.

Your Turn!

1) $3, 2, 4, 8, 3, 10$

Mode: _____   Range: _____

Mean: _____   Median: _____

2) $6, 3, 2, 9, 5, 7, 2, 14$

Mode: _____   Range: _____

Mean: _____   Median: _____

3) $5, 4, 3, 2, 9, 5, 6, 8, 12$

Mode: _____   Range: _____

Mean: _____   Median: _____

4) $12, 6, 8, 6, 9, 6, 4, 13$

Mode: _____   Range: _____

Mean: _____   Median: _____

Name: .... **Date:** ....

Topic	Mean, Median, Mode, and Range of the Given Data - Answers
Notes	✓ Mean: $\dfrac{sum\ of\ the\ data}{total\ number\ of\ data\ entires}$ ✓ Mode: value in the list that appears most often. ✓ Median: is the middle number of a group of numbers that have been arranged in order by size. ✓ Range: the difference of largest value and smallest value in the list.
Example	**Find the mode and median of these numbers?** $16, 10, 6, 3, 1, 16, 2, 4$ **Solution:** Mode: value in the list that appears most often. Number 16 is the value in the list that appears most often (there are two number 16). To find median, write the numbers in order: $1, 2, 3, 4, 6, 10, 16, 16$ Number 4 and 6 are in the middle. Find their average: $\dfrac{4+6}{2} = \dfrac{10}{2} = 5$ The median is 5.
Your Turn!	1) $3, 2, 4, 8, 3, 10$ Mode: 3 Range: 8 Mean: 5 Median: 3.5 2) $6, 3, 2, 9, 5, 7, 2, 14$ Mode: 2 Range: 12 Mean: 6 Median: 5.5 3) $5, 4, 3, 2, 9, 5, 6, 8, 12$ Mode: 5 Range: 10 Mean: 6 Median: 5 4) $12, 6, 8, 6, 9, 6, 4, 13$ Mode: 6 Range: 9 Mean: 8 Median: 7

Name: .... **Date:** ....

Topic	Probability Problems
Notes	✓ Probability is the likelihood of something happening in the future. It is expressed as a number between zero (can never happen) to 1 (will always happen). ✓ Probability can be expressed as a fraction, a decimal, or a percent. ✓ Probability formula: $Probability = \dfrac{number\ of\ desired\ outcomes}{number\ of\ total\ outcomes}$
Example	*If there are 3 green balls, 4 red balls, and 10 blue balls in a basket, what is the probability that Jason will pick out a red ball from the basket?* **Solution:** There are 4 red ball and 17 are total number of balls. Therefore, probability that Jason will pick out a red ball from the basket is 4 out of 17 or $\dfrac{4}{3+4+10} = \dfrac{4}{17}$
Your Turn!	1) A number is chosen at random from 1 to 20. Find the probability of selecting a prime number. (A prime number is a whole number that is only divisible by itself and 1) _____ 2) There are only red and blue cards in a box. The probability of choosing a red card in the box at random is one third. If there are 24 blue cards, how many cards are in the box? _____ 3) A die is rolled, what is the probability that an even number is obtained? _____

Name:	Date: ....

Topic	**Probability Problems - Answers**	
Notes	✓ Probability is the likelihood of something happening in the future. It is expressed as a number between zero (can never happen) to 1 (will always happen). ✓ Probability can be expressed as a fraction, a decimal, or a percent. ✓ Probability formula: $Probability = \dfrac{number\ of\ desired\ outcomes}{number\ of\ total\ outcomes}$	
Example	***If there are 3 green balls, 4 red balls, and 10 blue balls in a basket, what is the probability that Jason will pick out a red ball from the basket?*** **Solution:** There are 4 red ball and 17 are total number of balls. Therefore, probability that Jason will pick out a red ball from the basket is 4 out of 17 or $\dfrac{4}{3+4+10} = \dfrac{4}{17}$	
Your Turn!	1) A number is chosen at random from 1 to 20. Find the probability of selecting a prime number. (A prime number is a whole number that is only divisible by itself and 1) $\dfrac{8}{20} = \dfrac{2}{5}$ *(There are 8 prime numbers from 1 to 20: 2, 3, 5, 7, 11, 13, 17, 19)*	
	2) There are only red and blue cards in a box. The probability of choosing a red card in the box at random is one third. If there are 24 blue cards, how many cards are in the box? 36	
	3) A die is rolled, what is the probability that an even number is obtained? $\dfrac{1}{2}$	

Name: .... Date: ....

Topic	**Pie Graph**
Notes	✓ A Pie Chart is a circle chart divided into sectors, each sector represents the relative size of each value.

Example	A library has 460 books that include Mathematics, Physics, Chemistry, English and History. Use following graph to answer the question. **What is the number of Physics books?** **Solution:** Number of total books = 460 Percent of Physics books = 25% = 0.25 Then, umber of Physics books: $0.25 \times 460 = 115$

Your Turn!

The circle graph below shows all Mr. Smith's expenses for last month. Mr. Smith spent $440 for clothes last month.

Mr. Smith's last month expenses

1) How much did Mr. Smith spend for his Books last month? _____

2) How much did Mr. Smith spend for Bills last month? _____

3) How much did Mr. Smith spend for his foods last month? _____

Name:	Date: ....

Topic	**Pie Graph**
Notes	✓ A Pie Chart is a circle chart divided into sectors, each sector represents the relative size of each value.

Example	A library has 460 books that include Mathematics, Physics, Chemistry, English and History. Use following graph to answer the question. **What is the number of Physics books?** **Solution:** Number of total books $= 460$ Percent of Physics books $= 25\% = 0.25$ Then, umber of Physics books: $$0.25 \times 460 = 115$$ History 10% Mathematics 30% English 15% Chemistry 20% Physics 25%

Your Turn!	The circle graph below shows all Mr. Smith's expenses for last month. Mr. Smith spent $440 for clothes last month. Bills 18% Foods 25% Others 23% Clothes 20% Books 14% Mr. Smith's last month expenses
	1) How much did Mr. Smith spend for his Books last month? $308
	2) How much did Mr. Smith spend for Bills last month? $396
	3) How much did Mr. Smith spend for his foods last month? $550

| Name: .... | Date: .... |

Topic	**Permutations and Combinations**
Notes	✓ Permutations: The number of ways to choose a sample of k elements from a set of n distinct objects where order does matter, and replacements are not allowed. For a permutation problem, use this formula: $$_nP_k = \frac{n!}{(n-k)!}$$ ✓ Combination: The number of ways to choose a sample of r elements from a set of n distinct objects where order does not matter, and replacements are not allowed. For a combination problem, use this formula: $$_nC_r = \frac{n!}{r!\,(n-r)!}$$ ✓ Factorials are products, indicated by an exclamation mark. For example, 4! Equals: $4 \times 3 \times 2 \times 1$. Remember that 0! is defined to be equal to 1.
Example	***How many ways can we pick a team of 4 people from a group of 8?*** **Solution:** Since the order doesn't matter, we need to use combination formula where n is 8 and r is 4. Then: $\frac{n!}{r!\,(n-r)!} = \frac{8!}{4!\,(8-4)!} = \frac{8!}{4!\,(4)!} = \frac{8\times7\times6\times5\times4!}{4!\,(4)!} = \frac{8\times7\times6\times5}{4\times3\times2\times1} = \frac{1,680}{24} = 70$
Your Turn!	1) In how many ways can 8 athletes be arranged in a straight line? _____
	2) How many ways can we award a first and second place prize among eight contestants? _____
	3) In how many ways can we choose 3 players from a team of 9 players? _____

Name:	Date: ....

Topic	**Permutations and Combinations - Answers**
Notes	✓ Permutations: The number of ways to choose a sample of k elements from a set of n distinct objects where order does matter, and replacements are not allowed. For a permutation problem, use this formula: $$_nP_k = \frac{n!}{(n-k)!}$$ ✓ Combination: The number of ways to choose a sample of r elements from a set of n distinct objects where order does not matter, and replacements are not allowed. For a combination problem, use this formula: $$_nC_r = \frac{n!}{r!\,(n-r)!}$$ ✓ Factorials are products, indicated by an exclamation mark. For example, 4! Equals: $4 \times 3 \times 2 \times 1$. Remember that 0! is defined to be equal to 1.
Example	***How many ways can we pick a team of 4 people from a group of 8?*** **Solution:** Since the order doesn't matter, we need to use combination formula where n is 8 and r is 4. Then: $\frac{n!}{r!\,(n-r)!} = \frac{8!}{4!\,(8-4)!} = \frac{8!}{4!\,(4)!} = \frac{8 \times 7 \times 6 \times 5 \times 4!}{4!\,(4)!} = \frac{8 \times 7 \times 6 \times 5}{4 \times 3 \times 2 \times 1} = \frac{1,680}{24} = 70$
Your Turn!	1) In how many ways can 8 athletes be arranged in a straight line? 40,320
	2) How many ways can we award a first and second place prize among eight contestants? 56
	3) In how many ways can we choose 3 players from a team of 9 players? 84

Name: ....   **Date:** ....

Topic	**Function Notation and Evaluation**
Notes	✓ Functions are mathematical operations that assign unique outputs to given inputs. ✓ Function notation is the way a function is written. It is meant to be a precise way of giving information about the function without a rather lengthy written explanation. ✓ The most popular function notation is $f(x)$ which is read "f of x". ✓ To evaluate a function, plug in the input (the given value or expression) for the function's variable (place holder, x).
Example	**Evaluate**: $h(n) = 2n^2 - 2$, find $h(2)$. **Solution:** Substitute n with 2: Then: $h(n) = 2n^2 - 2 \rightarrow h(2) = 2(2)^2 - 2 = 8 - 2 \rightarrow h(2) = 6$

Your Turn!	1) $f(x) = x - 2$, find $f(-1)$ _____	2) $g(x) = 2x + 4$, find $g(3)$ _____
	3) $g(n) = 2n - 8$, find $g(-1)$ _____	4) $h(n) = n^2 - 1$, find $h(-2)$ _____
	5) $f(x) = x^2 + 12$, find $f(5)$ _____	6) $g(x) = 2x^2 - 9$, find $g(-2)$ _____
	7) $w(x) = 2x^2 - 4x$, find $w(2n)$ _____	8) $p(x) = 4x^3 - 10$, find $p(-3a)$ _____

| Name: .... | Date: .... |

Topic	**Function Notation and Evaluation - Answers**
Notes	✓ Functions are mathematical operations that assign unique outputs to given inputs. ✓ Function notation is the way a function is written. It is meant to be a precise way of giving information about the function without a rather lengthy written explanation. ✓ The most popular function notation is $f(x)$ which is read "f of x". ✓ To evaluate a function, plug in the input (the given value or expression) for the function's variable (place holder, x).
Example	**Evaluate**: $h(n) = 2n^2 - 2$, find $h(2)$. **Solution:** Substitute n with 2: Then: $h(n) = 2n^2 - 2 \rightarrow h(2) = 2(2)^2 - 2 = 8 - 2 \rightarrow h(2) = 6$

Your Turn!	1) $f(x) = x - 2$, find $f(-1)$ $f(-1) = -3$	2) $g(x) = 2x + 4$, find $g(3)$ $g(3) = 10$
	3) $g(n) = 2n - 8$, find $g(-1)$ $g(-1) = -10$	4) $h(n) = n^2 - 1$, find $h(-2)$ $h(-2) = 3$
	5) $f(x) = x^2 + 12$, find $f(5)$ $f(5) = 37$	6) $g(x) = 2x^2 - 9$, find $g(-2)$ $g(-2) = -1$
	7) $w(x) = 2x^2 - 4x$, find $w(2n)$ $w(2n) = 8n^2 - 8n$	8) $p(x) = 4x^3 - 10$, find $p(-3a)$ $p(-3a) = -108a^3 + 30a$

Name:	**Date:** ....

Topic	**Adding and Subtracting Functions**
Notes	✓ Just like we can add and subtract numbers and expressions, we can add or subtract two functions and simplify or evaluate them. The result is a new function. ✓ For two functions $f(x)$ and $g(x)$, we can create two new functions: $(f + g)(x) = f(x) + g(x)$ and $(f - g)(x) = f(x) - g(x)$
Example	$g(a) = 2a - 5, f(a) = a + 8,$ Find: $(g + f)(a)$ **Solution:** $(g + f)(a) = g(a) + f(a)$ Then: $(g + f)(a) = (2a - 5) + (a + 8) = 3a + 3$

Your Turn!	1) $g(x) = x - 2$ $h(x) = 2x + 6$ Find: $(h + g)(3)$ _____	2) $f(x) = 3x + 2$ $g(x) = -x - 6$ Find: $(f + g)(2)$ _____
	3) $f(x) = 5x + 8$ $g(x) = 3x - 12$ Find: $(f - g)(-2)$ _____	4) $h(x) = 2x^2 - 10$ $g(x) = 3x + 12$ Find: $(h + g)(3)$ _____
	5) $g(x) = 12x - 8$ $h(x) = 3x^2 + 14$ Find: $(h - g)(x)$ _____	6) $h(x) = -2x^2 - 18$ $g(x) = 4x^2 + 15$ Find: $(h - g)(a)$ _____

Name:	Date: ....

Topic	Adding and Subtracting Functions - Answers
Notes	✓ Just like we can add and subtract numbers and expressions, we can add or subtract two functions and simplify or evaluate them. The result is a new function. ✓ For two functions $f(x)$ and $g(x)$, we can create two new functions: $(f + g)(x) = f(x) + g(x)$ and $(f - g)(x) = f(x) - g(x)$
Example	$g(a) = 2a - 5, f(a) = a + 8$, Find: $(g + f)(a)$ **Solution:** $(g + f)(a) = g(a) + f(a)$ Then: $(g + f)(a) = (2a - 5) + (a + 8) = 3a + 3$

Your Turn!	1) $g(x) = x - 2$ $h(x) = 2x + 6$ Find: $(h + g)(3)$ 13	2) $f(x) = 3x + 2$ $g(x) = -x - 6$ Find: $(f + g)(2)$ 0
	3) $f(x) = 5x + 8$ $g(x) = 3x - 12$ Find: $(f - g)(-2)$ 16	4) $h(x) = 2x^2 - 10$ $g(x) = 3x + 12$ Find: $(h + g)(3)$ 29
	5) $g(x) = 12x - 8$ $h(x) = 3x^2 + 14$ Find: $(h - g)(x)$ $3x^2 - 12x + 22$	6) $h(x) = -2x^2 - 18$ $g(x) = 4x^2 + 15$ Find: $(h - g)(a)$ $-6a^2 - 33$

| Name: .... | | Date: .... |

Topic	**Multiplying and Dividing Functions**
Notes	✓ Just like we can multiply and divide numbers and expressions, we can multiply and divide two functions and simplify or evaluate them. ✓ For two functions $f(x)$ and $g(x)$, we can create two new functions: $(f.g)(x) = f(x).g(x)$ and $\left(\frac{f}{g}\right)(x) = \frac{f(x)}{g(x)}$
Example	$g(x) = x + 5, f(x) = x - 3,$ Find: $(g.f)(2)$ **Solution:** $(g.f)(x) = g(x).f(x) = (x+5)(x-3) = x^2 - 3x + 5x - 15 = x^2 + 2x - 15$ Substitute x with 2: $(g.f)(x) = (2)^2 + 2(2) - 15 = 4 + 4 - 15 = -7$

Your Turn!	1) $g(x) = x - 5$ $h(x) = x + 6$ Find: $(g.h)(-1)$ _____	2) $f(x) = 2x + 2$ $g(x) = -x - 6$ Find: $(\frac{f}{g})(-2)$ _____
	3) $f(x) = 5x + 3$ $g(x) = 2x - 4$ Find: $(\frac{f}{g})(5)$ _____	4) $h(x) = x^2 - 2$ $g(x) = x + 4$ Find: $(g.h)(3)$ _____
	5) $g(x) = 4x - 12$ $h(x) = x^2 + 4$ Find: $(g.h)(-2)$ _____	6) $h(x) = 3x^2 - 8$ $g(x) = 4x + 6$ Find: $(\frac{f}{g})(-4)$ _____

Name:	Date: ....

Topic	**Multiplying and Dividing Functions - Answers**	
Notes	✓ Just like we can multiply and divide numbers and expressions, we can multiply and divide two functions and simplify or evaluate them. ✓ For two functions $f(x)$ and $g(x)$, we can create two new functions: $(f.g)(x) = f(x).g(x)$ and $\left(\frac{f}{g}\right)(x) = \frac{f(x)}{g(x)}$	
Example	$g(x) = x + 5, f(x) = x - 3$, Find: $(g.f)(2)$ **Solution:** $(g.f)(x) = g(x).f(x) = (x+5)(x-3) = x^2 - 3x + 5x - 15 = x^2 + 2x - 15$ Substitute x with 2: $(g.f)(x) = (2)^2 + 2(2) - 15 = 4 + 4 - 15 = -7$	
Your Turn!	1) $g(x) = x - 5$ $h(x) = x + 6$ Find: $(g.h)(-1)$ $(g.h)(-1) = -30$	2) $f(x) = 2x + 2$ $g(x) = -x - 6$ Find: $\left(\frac{f}{g}\right)(-2)$ $\left(\frac{f}{g}\right)(-2) = \frac{1}{2}$
	3) $f(x) = 5x + 3$ $g(x) = 2x - 4$ Find: $\left(\frac{f}{g}\right)(5)$ $\left(\frac{f}{g}\right)(5) = \frac{14}{3}$	4) $h(x) = x^2 - 2$ $g(x) = x + 4$ Find: $(g.h)(3)$ $(g.h)(3) = 49$
	5) $g(x) = 4x - 12$ $h(x) = x^2 + 4$ Find: $(g.h)(-2)$ $(g.h)(-2) = -160$	6) $h(x) = 3x^2 - 8$ $g(x) = 4x + 6$ Find: $\left(\frac{f}{g}\right)(-4)$ $\left(\frac{f}{g}\right)(-4) = -4$

Name: .... **Date:** ....

Topic	**Composition of Functions**
Notes	✓ "Composition of functions" simply means combining two or more functions in a way where the output from one function becomes the input for the next function. ✓ The notation used for composition is: $(f o g)(x) = f(g(x))$ and is read "f composed with g of x" or "f of g of x".
Example	*Using* $f(x) = x - 8$ *and* $g(x) = x + 2$, *find:* $(f o g)(3)$ **Solution:** $(f o g)(x) = f(g(x))$ *Then:* $(f o g)(x) = f(g(x)) = f(x + 2) = x + 2 - 8 = x - 6$ Substitute x with 3: $(f o g)(3) = f(g(3)) = 3 - 6 = -3$
Your Turn!	1) $f(x) = 2x$ $g(x) = x + 3$ Find: $(fog)(2)$ _____ 3) $f(x) = 3x$ $g(x) = x + 4$ Find: $(gof)(4)$ _____ 5) $f(x) = 2x - 8$ $g(x) = x + 10$ Find: $(fog)(-2)$ _____

2) $f(x) = x + 2$

$g(x) = x - 6$
Find: $(fog)(-1)$

_____

4) $h(x) = 2x - 2$

$g(x) = x + 4$
Find: $(goh)(2)$

_____

6) $f(x) = x^2 - 8$

$g(x) = 2x + 3$
Find: $(gof)(4)$

_____

Name:	Date: ....

Topic	**Composition of Functions - Answers**
Notes	✓ "Composition of functions" simply means combining two or more functions in a way where the output from one function becomes the input for the next function. ✓ The notation used for composition is: $(f o g)(x) = f(g(x))$ and is read "f composed with g of x" or "f of g of x".
Example	**Using** $f(x) = x - 8$ **and** $g(x) = x + 2$, **find:** $(f \ o \ g)(3)$ **Solution:** $(f \ o \ g)(x) = f(g(x))$ **Then:** $(f \ o \ g)(x) = f(g(x)) = f(x + 2) = x + 2 - 8 = x - 6$ Substitute x with 3: $(f \ o \ g)(3) = f(g(3)) = 3 - 6 = -3$

Your Turn!	1) $f(x) = 2x$ $g(x) = x + 3$ Find: $(fog)(2)$ 10	2) $f(x) = x + 2$ $g(x) = x - 6$ Find: $(fog)(-1)$ -5
	3) $f(x) = 3x$ $g(x) = x + 4$ Find: $(gof)(4)$ 16	4) $h(x) = 2x - 2$ $g(x) = x + 4$ Find: $(goh)(2)$ 6
	5) $f(x) = 2x - 8$ $g(x) = x + 10$ Find: $(fog)(-2)$ 8	6) $f(x) = x^2 - 8$ $g(x) = 2x + 3$ Find: $(gof)(4)$ 19

SHSAT Test Review

The Specialized High School Admissions Test, commonly known as the SHSAT, is a standardized test that is administered by the New York City Department of Education. SHSAT is the criterion for admissions to New York City Specialized High Schools. It is available to 8th grade students in New York City. 9th grade students may also choose to take the 9th grade version of the SHSAT.

The SHSAT assesses English Comprehension (Verbal) and Mathematics knowledge and skills.

The Mathematics section of the test is a 75-minute test that covers basic mathematics topics, quantitative problem-solving and algebraic questions. There are 5 Gridded-Response and 52 multiple choice questions in the Math section of SHSAT and students have 75 minutes to complete this section. Calculator is NOT allowed for the SHSAT test.

In this book, we have covered all Mathematics topics students need to know. Now, it's time to take a real SHSAT Math test. In this section, there are two complete SHSAT Mathematics Tests. Take these tests to see what score you'll be able to receive on a real SHSAT test.

Good luck!

Time to Test

Time to refine your Mathematics skill with a practice test

In this section, there are two complete SHSAT Mathematics practice tests. Take these tests to simulate the test day experience. After you've finished, score your tests using the answer keys.

Before You Start

- You'll need a pencil and a timer to take the test.

- It's okay to guess. There is no penalty for wrong answers.

- Use the answer sheet provided to record your answers.

- After you've finished the test, review the answer key to see where you went wrong.

- For each multiple-choice question, there are four possible answers. Choose which one is best. For grids in questions, write your answer in the answer boxes at the top of the grid. Then, as shown below fill in a bubble under each box in which you wrote your answer.

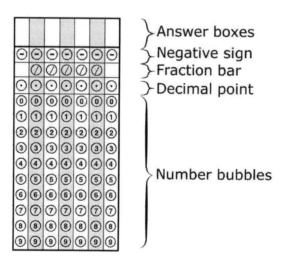

Good Luck!

SHSAT Practice Tests Answer Sheet

Remove (or photocopy) these answer sheets and use them to complete the practice tests.

SHSAT Practice Test 1: Grid-ins Questions Answer Sheet

1

2

3

4

5

SHSAT Practice Test 1 – Multiple Choice Questions Answer Sheet

6	Ⓐ Ⓑ Ⓒ Ⓓ	18	Ⓐ Ⓑ Ⓒ Ⓓ	30	Ⓐ Ⓑ Ⓒ Ⓓ	42	Ⓐ Ⓑ Ⓒ Ⓓ	54	Ⓐ Ⓑ Ⓒ Ⓓ
7	Ⓐ Ⓑ Ⓒ Ⓓ	19	Ⓐ Ⓑ Ⓒ Ⓓ	31	Ⓐ Ⓑ Ⓒ Ⓓ	43	Ⓐ Ⓑ Ⓒ Ⓓ	55	Ⓐ Ⓑ Ⓒ Ⓓ
8	Ⓐ Ⓑ Ⓒ Ⓓ	20	Ⓐ Ⓑ Ⓒ Ⓓ	32	Ⓐ Ⓑ Ⓒ Ⓓ	44	Ⓐ Ⓑ Ⓒ Ⓓ	56	Ⓐ Ⓑ Ⓒ Ⓓ
9	Ⓐ Ⓑ Ⓒ Ⓓ	21	Ⓐ Ⓑ Ⓒ Ⓓ	33	Ⓐ Ⓑ Ⓒ Ⓓ	45	Ⓐ Ⓑ Ⓒ Ⓓ	57	Ⓐ Ⓑ Ⓒ Ⓓ
10	Ⓐ Ⓑ Ⓒ Ⓓ	22	Ⓐ Ⓑ Ⓒ Ⓓ	34	Ⓐ Ⓑ Ⓒ Ⓓ	46	Ⓐ Ⓑ Ⓒ Ⓓ		
11	Ⓐ Ⓑ Ⓒ Ⓓ	23	Ⓐ Ⓑ Ⓒ Ⓓ	35	Ⓐ Ⓑ Ⓒ Ⓓ	47	Ⓐ Ⓑ Ⓒ Ⓓ		
12	Ⓐ Ⓑ Ⓒ Ⓓ	24	Ⓐ Ⓑ Ⓒ Ⓓ	36	Ⓐ Ⓑ Ⓒ Ⓓ	48	Ⓐ Ⓑ Ⓒ Ⓓ		
13	Ⓐ Ⓑ Ⓒ Ⓓ	25	Ⓐ Ⓑ Ⓒ Ⓓ	37	Ⓐ Ⓑ Ⓒ Ⓓ	49	Ⓐ Ⓑ Ⓒ Ⓓ		
14	Ⓐ Ⓑ Ⓒ Ⓓ	26	Ⓐ Ⓑ Ⓒ Ⓓ	38	Ⓐ Ⓑ Ⓒ Ⓓ	50	Ⓐ Ⓑ Ⓒ Ⓓ		
15	Ⓐ Ⓑ Ⓒ Ⓓ	27	Ⓐ Ⓑ Ⓒ Ⓓ	39	Ⓐ Ⓑ Ⓒ Ⓓ	51	Ⓐ Ⓑ Ⓒ Ⓓ		
16	Ⓐ Ⓑ Ⓒ Ⓓ	28	Ⓐ Ⓑ Ⓒ Ⓓ	40	Ⓐ Ⓑ Ⓒ Ⓓ	52	Ⓐ Ⓑ Ⓒ Ⓓ		
17	Ⓐ Ⓑ Ⓒ Ⓓ	29	Ⓐ Ⓑ Ⓒ Ⓓ	41	Ⓐ Ⓑ Ⓒ Ⓓ	53	Ⓐ Ⓑ Ⓒ Ⓓ		

SHSAT Practice Test 2: Grid-ins Questions Answer Sheet

1

2

3

4

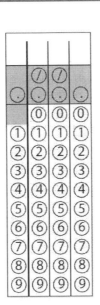

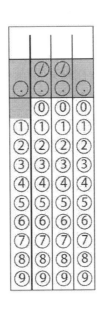

5

SHSAT Practice Test 2 – Multiple Choice Questions Answer Sheet

6	Ⓐ Ⓑ Ⓒ Ⓓ	18	Ⓐ Ⓑ Ⓒ Ⓓ	30	Ⓐ Ⓑ Ⓒ Ⓓ	42	Ⓐ Ⓑ Ⓒ Ⓓ	54	Ⓐ Ⓑ Ⓒ Ⓓ
7	Ⓐ Ⓑ Ⓒ Ⓓ	19	Ⓐ Ⓑ Ⓒ Ⓓ	31	Ⓐ Ⓑ Ⓒ Ⓓ	43	Ⓐ Ⓑ Ⓒ Ⓓ	55	Ⓐ Ⓑ Ⓒ Ⓓ
8	Ⓐ Ⓑ Ⓒ Ⓓ	20	Ⓐ Ⓑ Ⓒ Ⓓ	32	Ⓐ Ⓑ Ⓒ Ⓓ	44	Ⓐ Ⓑ Ⓒ Ⓓ	56	Ⓐ Ⓑ Ⓒ Ⓓ
9	Ⓐ Ⓑ Ⓒ Ⓓ	21	Ⓐ Ⓑ Ⓒ Ⓓ	33	Ⓐ Ⓑ Ⓒ Ⓓ	45	Ⓐ Ⓑ Ⓒ Ⓓ	57	Ⓐ Ⓑ Ⓒ Ⓓ
10	Ⓐ Ⓑ Ⓒ Ⓓ	22	Ⓐ Ⓑ Ⓒ Ⓓ	34	Ⓐ Ⓑ Ⓒ Ⓓ	46	Ⓐ Ⓑ Ⓒ Ⓓ		
11	Ⓐ Ⓑ Ⓒ Ⓓ	23	Ⓐ Ⓑ Ⓒ Ⓓ	35	Ⓐ Ⓑ Ⓒ Ⓓ	47	Ⓐ Ⓑ Ⓒ Ⓓ		
12	Ⓐ Ⓑ Ⓒ Ⓓ	24	Ⓐ Ⓑ Ⓒ Ⓓ	36	Ⓐ Ⓑ Ⓒ Ⓓ	48	Ⓐ Ⓑ Ⓒ Ⓓ		
13	Ⓐ Ⓑ Ⓒ Ⓓ	25	Ⓐ Ⓑ Ⓒ Ⓓ	37	Ⓐ Ⓑ Ⓒ Ⓓ	49	Ⓐ Ⓑ Ⓒ Ⓓ		
14	Ⓐ Ⓑ Ⓒ Ⓓ	26	Ⓐ Ⓑ Ⓒ Ⓓ	38	Ⓐ Ⓑ Ⓒ Ⓓ	50	Ⓐ Ⓑ Ⓒ Ⓓ		
15	Ⓐ Ⓑ Ⓒ Ⓓ	27	Ⓐ Ⓑ Ⓒ Ⓓ	39	Ⓐ Ⓑ Ⓒ Ⓓ	51	Ⓐ Ⓑ Ⓒ Ⓓ		
16	Ⓐ Ⓑ Ⓒ Ⓓ	28	Ⓐ Ⓑ Ⓒ Ⓓ	40	Ⓐ Ⓑ Ⓒ Ⓓ	52	Ⓐ Ⓑ Ⓒ Ⓓ		
17	Ⓐ Ⓑ Ⓒ Ⓓ	29	Ⓐ Ⓑ Ⓒ Ⓓ	41	Ⓐ Ⓑ Ⓒ Ⓓ	53	Ⓐ Ⓑ Ⓒ Ⓓ		

SHSAT Mathematics

Practice Test 1

57 questions

Total time for this section: 75 Minutes

You may NOT use a calculator on this Test.

1) In the figure below, what is the value of x?

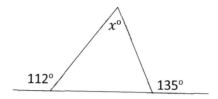

2) In the following right triangle, if the sides AB and AC become twice longer, what will be the ratio of the perimeter of the triangle to its area?

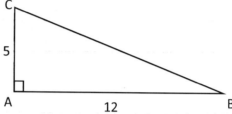

3) $-18 + 6 \times (-5) - [4 + 22 \times (-4)] \div 2 + 8 = ?$

4) If $\frac{x-3}{5} = N$ and $N = 6$, what is the value of x?

5) A construction company is building a wall. The company can build 30 cm of the wall per minute. After 40 minutes $\frac{3}{4}$ of the wall is completed. How many meters is the wall?

6) When a number is subtracted from 24 and the difference is divided by that number, the result is 3. What is the value of the number?

    A. 2

    B. 4

    C. 6

    D. 12

7) An angle is equal to one ninth of its supplement. What is the measure of that angle?

    A. 18

    B. 24

    C. 36

    D. 45

8) John traveled 150 km in 6 hours and Alice traveled 180 km in 4 hours. What is the ratio of the average speed of John to average speed of Alice?

    A. 3 : 2

    B. 2 : 3

    C. 5 : 9

    D. 5 : 6

9) If the area of the following rectangular $ABCD$ is 100, and E is the midpoint of AB, what is the area of the shaded part?

    A. 25

    B. 50

    C. 75

    D. 80

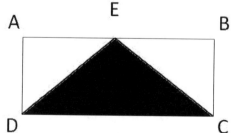

10) A taxi driver earns $9 per 1-hour work. If he works 10 hours a day and in 1 hour he uses 2-liters petrol with price $1 for 1-liter. How much money does he earn in one day?

    A. $90

    B. $88

    C. $70

    D. $60

Use the chart below to answer the question.

Color	Number
White	20
Black	30
Beige	40

11) There are also purple marbles in the bag. Which of the following can NOT be the probability of randomly selecting a purple marble from the bag?

    A. $\dfrac{1}{10}$

    B. $\dfrac{1}{4}$

    C. $\dfrac{2}{5}$

    D. $\dfrac{7}{15}$

12) Find the average of the following numbers: 17, 13, 7, 21, 22

    A. 17

    B. 16.5

    C. 16

    D. 11

13) The sum of six different negative integers is -70. If the smallest of these integers is -15, what is the largest possible value of one of the other five integers?

    A. -14
    B. -10
    C. -5
    D. -1

14) If $3x - 5 = 8.5$, What is the value of $5x + 3$?

    A. 13
    B. 15.5
    C. 20.5
    D. 25.5

15) The price of a sofa is decreased by 15% to $476. What was its original price?

    A. $480

    B. $520

    C. $560

    D. $600

16) Right triangle ABC has two legs of lengths 9 cm (AB) and 12 cm (AC). What is the length of the third side (BC)?

    A. 6 cm

    B. 8 cm

    C. 14 cm

    D. 15 cm

Questions 15 to 17 are based on the following data

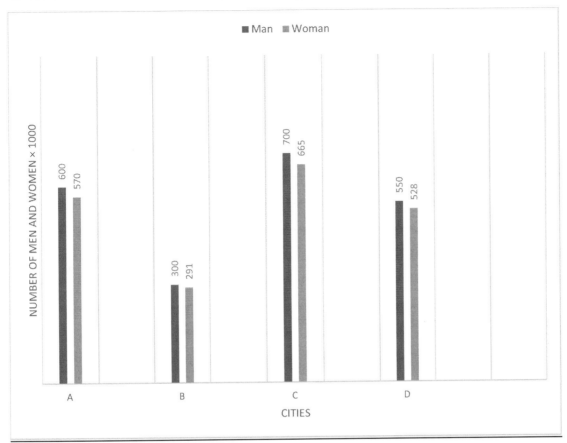

17) What's the maximum ratio of woman to man in the four cities?

    A. 0.98

    B. 0.97

    C. 0.96

    D. 0.95

18) What's the ratio of percentage of men in city A to percentage of women in city C?

    A. 0.9

    B. 0.95

    C. 1

    D. 1.05

19) How many women should be added to city D until the ratio of women to men will be 1.2?

    A. 120
    B. 128
    C. 132
    D. 160

20) If 40% of a class are girls, and 25% of girls play tennis, what percent of the class play tennis?

    A. 10%

    B. 15%

    C. 20%

    D. 40%

21) The area of a circle is less than 64 π. Which of the following can be the circumference of the circle? (Select one or more answer choices)

    A. 12 π

    B. 16 π

    C. 24 π

    D. 32 π

22) Which of the following values for x and y satisfy the following system of equations?

$$\begin{cases} x + 4y = 10 \\ 5x + 10y = 20 \end{cases}$$

    A. $x = 3, y = 2$
    B. $x = 2, y - 3$
    C. $x = -2, y = 3$
    D. $x = 3, y = -2$

23) If 60% of A is 20% of B, then B is what percent of A?

    A. 3%

    B. 30%

    C. 200%

    D. 300%

24) In the figure, MN is 40 cm. How long is ON?

    A. 25 cm
    B. 20 cm
    C. 15 cm
    D. 10 cm

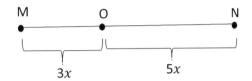

25) The price of a car was $20,000 in 2014, $16,000 in 2015 and $12,800 in 2016. What is the rate of depreciation of the price of car per year?

    A. 15%

    B. 20%

    C. 25%

    D. 30%

26) The width of a box is one third of its length. The height of the box is one third of its width. If the length of the box is 27 cm, what is the volume of the box?

    A. 81 cm^3

    B. 162 cm^3

    C. 243 cm^3

    D. 729 cm^3

27) How many possible outfit combinations come from six shirts, three slacks, and five ties?

    A. 15
    B. 18
    C. 30
    D. 90

28) A bank is offering 4.5% simple interest on a savings account. If you deposit $8,000, how much interest will you earn in five years?

    A. $360

    B. $720

    C. $1,800

    D. $3,600

Gender	Under 45	45 or older	total
Male	12	6	18
Female	5	7	12
Total	17	13	30

29) The table above shows the distribution of age and gender for 30 employees in a company. If one employee is selected at random, what is the probability that the employee selected be either a female under age 45 or a male age 45 or older?

    A. $\dfrac{5}{6}$

    B. $\dfrac{5}{30}$

    C. $\dfrac{6}{30}$

    D. $\dfrac{11}{30}$

30) The cost, in thousands of dollars, of producing x thousands of textbooks is
$C(x) = x^2 + 2x$. The revenue, also in thousands of dollars, is $R(x) = 40x$. find the profit or loss if 30 textbooks are produced. (profit = revenue − cost)

A. $2,160 profit

B. $240 profit

C. $2,160 loss

D. $240 loss

31) What is the length of AB in the following figure if $AE = 4$, $CD = 6$ and $AC = 12$?
   A. 3.8
   B. 4.8
   C. 7.2
   D. 24

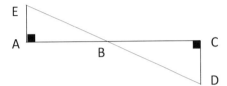

32) If the area of trapezoid is 126 cm, what is the perimeter of the trapezoid?

   A. 12 cm
   B. 32 cm
   C. 46 cm
   D. 55 cm

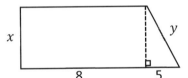

33) In five successive hours, a car travels 40 km, 45 km, 50 km, 35 km and 55 km. In the next five hours, it travels with an average speed of 50 km per hour. Find the total distance the car traveled in 10 hours.

A. 425 km

B. 450 km

C. 475 km

D.500 km

34) How long does a 420–miles trip take moving at 50 miles per hour (mph)?

    A. 4 hours

    B. 6 hours and 24 minutes

    C. 8 hours and 24 minutes

    D. 8 hours and 30 minutes

35) If 5 inches on a map represents an actual distance of 100 feet, then what actual distance does 18 inches on the map represent?

    A. 18

    B. 100

    C. 250

    D. 360

36) Two third of 18 is equal to $\frac{2}{5}$ of what number?

    A. 12

    B. 20

    C. 30

    D. 60

37) The marked price of a computer is D dollar. Its price decreased by 20% in January and later increased by 10% in February. What is the final price of the computer in D dollar?

    A. 0.80 D

    B. 0.88 D

    C. 0.90 D

    D. 1.20 D

38) A $40 shirt now selling for $28 is discounted by what percent?

    A. 20%

    B. 30%

    C. 40%

    D. 60%

39) Which of the following could be the product of two consecutive prime numbers?

    A. 2

    B. 10

    C. 14

    D. 15

40) Which of the following lists shows the fractions in order from least to greatest?
$$\frac{3}{4}, \frac{2}{7}, \frac{3}{8}, \frac{5}{11}$$

    A. $\frac{3}{8}, \frac{2}{7}, \frac{3}{4}, \frac{5}{11}$

    B. $\frac{2}{7}, \frac{5}{11}, \frac{3}{8}, \frac{3}{4}$

    C. $\frac{2}{7}, \frac{3}{8}, \frac{5}{11}, \frac{3}{4}$

    D. $\frac{3}{8}, \frac{2}{7}, \frac{5}{11}, \frac{3}{4}$

41) A boat sails 40 miles south and then 30 miles east. How far is the boat from its start point?

    A. 45 miles

    B. 50 miles

    C. 60 miles

    D. 70 miles

42) The ratio of boys and girls in a class is 4:7. If there are 44 students in the class, how many more boys should be enrolled to make the ratio 1:1?

    A. 8

    B. 10

    C. 12

    D. 16

43) Sophia purchased a sofa for $530.40. The sofa is regularly priced at $624. What was the percent discount Sophia received on the sofa?

    A. 12%

    B. 15%

    C. 20%

    D. 25%

44) The score of Emma was half as that of Ava and the score of Mia was twice that of Ava. If the score of Mia was 60, what is the score of Emma?

    A. 12

    B. 15

    C. 20

    D. 30

45) A bag contains 18 balls: two green, five black, eight blue, a brown, a red and one white. If 17 balls are removed from the bag at random, what is the probability that a brown ball has been removed?

    A. $\dfrac{1}{9}$

    B. $\dfrac{1}{6}$

    C. $\dfrac{16}{17}$

    D. $\dfrac{17}{18}$

46) The average of five consecutive numbers is 38. What is the smallest number?

    A. 38

    B. 36

    C. 34

    D. 12

47) How many tiles of 8 cm² is needed to cover a floor of dimension 6 cm by 24 cm?

   A. 6

   B. 12

   C. 18

   D. 24

48) The following graph shows the mark of six students in mathematics. What is the mean (average) of the marks?

   A. 15

   B. 14.5

   C. 14

   D. 13.5

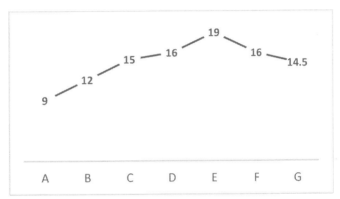

49) How many $\frac{1}{5}$ pound paperback books together weigh 50 pounds?

   A. 25

   B. 50

   C. 150

   D. 250

50) A rope weighs 600 grams per meter of length. What is the weight in kilograms of 12.2 meters of this rope? (1 kilograms = 1000 grams)

   A. 0.0732

   B. 0.732

   C. 7.32

   D. 73.20

51) A chemical solution contains 4% alcohol. If there is 24 ml of alcohol, what is the volume of the solution?

    A. 240 ml

    B. 480 ml

    C. 600 ml

    D. 1200 ml

52) What is the volume of the following square pyramid?
    A. 120 m^3
    B. 144 m^3
    C. 480 m^3
    D. 1440 m^3

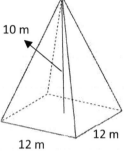

53) The average weight of 18 girls in a class is 60 kg and the average weight of 32 boys in the same class is 62 kg. What is the average weight of all the 50 students in that class?

    A. 60

    B. 61.28

    C. 61.68

    D. 62.90

54) The price of a laptop is decreased by 10% to $360. What is its original price?

    A. 320

    B. 380

    C. 400

    D. 450

55) What is the median of these numbers? 4, 9, 13, 8, 15, 18, 5

    A. 8

    B. 9

    C. 13

    D. 15

56) The surface area of a cylinder is $150\pi\ cm^2$. If its height is 10 cm, what is the radius of the cylinder?

    A. 13 cm

    B. 11 cm

    C. 15 cm

    D. 5 cm

57) In 1999, the average worker's income increased $2,000 per year starting from $24,000 annual salary. Which equation represents income greater than average? (I = income, x = number of years after 1999)

    A. $I > 2000\ x + 24000$

    B. $I > -2000\ x + 24000$

    C. $I < -2000\ x + 24000$

    D. $I < 2000\ x - 24000$

IF YOU FINISH BEFORE TIME IS CALLED, YOU MAY CHECK YOUR WORK ON THIS TEST.   STOP

SHSAT Mathematics

Practice Test 2

57 questions

Total time for this section: 75 Minutes

You may NOT use a calculator on this Test.

1) In the following shape, the area of the circle is 16π cm². What is the area of the square?

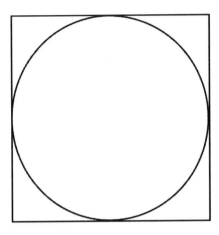

2) List A consists of the numbers {1, 3, 8, 10, 15}, and list B consists of the numbers {4, 6, 12, 14, 17}.

   If the two lists are combined, what is the median of the combined list?

3) A tree 32 feet tall casts a shadow 12 feet long. Jack is 6 feet tall. How long is Jack's shadow?

4) What is the value of the expression $3(x - 2y) + (2 - x)^2$ when $x = 5$ and $= -3$?

5) What is the value of x in the following equation? $-60 = 115 - x$

6) What's the area of the non-shaded part of the following figure?

A. 192

B. 152

C. 40

D. 42

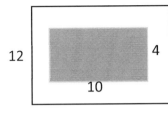

7) In the triangle below, if the measure of angle A is 37 degrees, then what is the value of y? (figure is NOT drawn to scale)

A. 62

B. 70

C. 78

D. 86

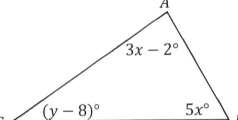

8) Simplify the expression.

$$(6x^3 - 8x^2 + 2x^4) - (4x^2 - 2x^4 + 2x^3)$$

A. $4x^4 + 4x^3 - 12x^2$

B. $4x^3 - 12x^2$

C. $4x^4 + 4x^3 - 12x^2$

D. $8x^3 - 12x^2$

Questions 9 and 11 are based on the following data

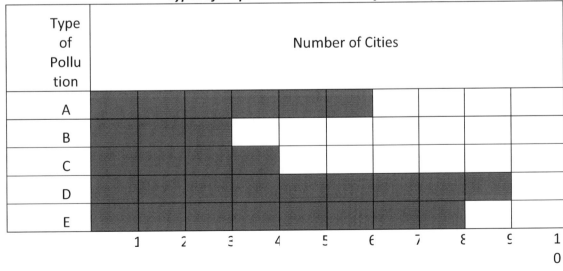

Types of air pollutions in 10 cities of a country

9) If a is the mean (average) of the number of cities in each pollution type category, b is the mode, and c is the median of the number of cities in each pollution type category, then which of the following must be true?

    A. $a < b < c$
    B. $b < a < c$
    C. $a = c$
    D. $b < c = a$

10) What percent of cities are in the type of pollution A, C, and E respectively?

    A. 60%, 40%, 90%
    B. 30%, 40%, 90%
    C. 30%, 40%, 60%
    D. 40%, 60%, 90%

11) How many cities should be added to type of pollutions B until the ratio of cities in type of pollution B to cities in type of pollution E will be 0.625?

    A. 2
    B. 3
    C. 4
    D. 5

12) There are only red and blue cards in a box. The probability of choosing a red card in the box at random is one third. If there are 246 blue cards, how many cards are in the box?

    A. 123
    B. 308
    C. 328
    D. 369

13) $\dfrac{1}{6b^2} + \dfrac{1}{6b} = \dfrac{1}{b^2}$, then b = ?

A. $-\dfrac{16}{15}$

B. 5

C. $-\dfrac{15}{16}$

D. 8

14) In two successive years, the population of a town is increased by 15% and 20%. What percent of the population is increased after two years?

A. 32%

B. 35%

C. 38%

D. 68%

15) Which of the following graphs represents the compound inequality $-2 \le 2x - 4 < 8$?

A.

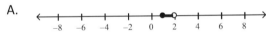

B.

C.

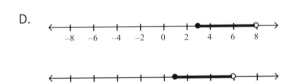

D.

16) What is the volume of a box with the following dimensions?

Hight = 4 cm   Width = 5 cm   Length = 6 cm

A. 15 cm³

B. 60 cm³

C. 90 cm³

D. 120 cm³

17) In the diagram below, circle A represents the set of all odd numbers, circle B represents the set of all negative numbers, and circle C represents the set of all multiples of 5. Which number could be replaced with y?

A. 5

B. 0

C. -5

D. -10

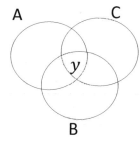

18) A basket contains 20 balls and the average weight of each of these balls is 25 g. The five heaviest balls have an average weight of 40 g each. If we remove the three heaviest balls from the basket, what is the average weight of the remaining balls?

A. 10

B. 20

C. 30

D. 35

19) Mr. Carlos family are choosing a menu for their reception. They have 3 choices of appetizers, 5 choices of entrees, 4 choices of cake. How many different menu combinations are possible for them to choose?

A. 12

B. 32

C. 60

D. 120

20) In a stadium the ratio of home fans to visiting fans in a crowd is 5:7. Which of the following could be the total number of fans in the stadium?

A. 12,324

B. 42,326

C. 44,566

D. 66,812

21) Last week 24,000 fans attended a football match. This week three times as many bought tickets, but one sixth of them cancelled their tickets. How many are attending this week?

   A. 48,000

   B. 54,000

   C. 60,000

   D. 72,000

22) What is the perimeter of a square in centimeters that has an area of 595.36 cm²?

   A. 97.6
   B. 96.2
   C. 95.7
   D. 92.6

23) A bread recipe calls for $2\frac{2}{3}$ cups of flour. If you only have $2\frac{5}{6}$ cups, how much more flour is needed?

   A. 1

   B. $\frac{1}{2}$

   C. 2

   D. $\frac{5}{6}$

24) The perimeter of a rectangular yard is 60 meters. What is its length if its width is twice its length?

   A. 10 meters

   B. 18 meters

   C. 20 meters

   D. 24 meters

25) Which of the following shows the numbers in descending order?

$$\frac{2}{3}, \ 0.68 \ , 67\% \ , \frac{4}{5}$$

A. 67%, 0.68, $\frac{2}{3}, \frac{4}{5}$

B. 67%, 0.68, $\frac{4}{5}, \frac{2}{3}$

C. 0.68, 67%, $\frac{2}{3} \ , \frac{4}{5}$

D. $\frac{2}{3}$, 67%, 0.68, $\frac{4}{5}$

26) The mean of 50 test scores was calculated as 88. But, it turned out that one of the scores was misread as 94 but it was 69. What is the correct mean of the test scores?

A. 85
B. 87
C. 87.5
D. 88.5

27) If Jim adds 100 stamps to his current stamp collection, the total number of stamps will be equal to $\frac{6}{5}$ the current number of stamps. If Jim adds 50% more stamps to the current collection, how many stamps will be in the collection?

A. 150
B. 300
C. 600
D. 750

28) Two dice are thrown simultaneously, what is the probability of getting a sum of 6 or 9?

A. $\frac{1}{3}$

B. $\frac{1}{4}$

C. $\frac{1}{6}$

D. $\frac{1}{12}$

29) A swimming pool holds 2,000 cubic feet of water. The swimming pool is 25 feet long and 10 feet wide. How deep is the swimming pool?

    A. 2
    B. 4
    C. 6
    D. 8

30) What is the area of a square whose diagonal is 8?

    A. 16

    B. 32

    C. 36

    D. 64

31) The sum of 8 numbers is greater than 240 and less than 320. Which of the following could be the average (arithmetic mean) of the numbers?

    A. 30
    B. 35
    C. 40
    D. 45

32) Anita's trick–or–treat bag contains 12 pieces of chocolate, 18 suckers, 18 pieces of gum, 24 pieces of licorice. If she randomly pulls a piece of candy from her bag, what is the probability of her pulling out a piece of sucker?

    A. $\dfrac{1}{3}$

    B. $\dfrac{1}{4}$

    C. $\dfrac{1}{6}$

    D. $\dfrac{1}{12}$

33) The average of 6 numbers is 12. The average of 4 of those numbers is 10. What is the average of the other two numbers.

    A. 10

    B. 12

    C. 14

    D. 16

34) In the following figure, point Q lies on line n, what is the value of y if $x = 35$?

    A. 15
    B. 25
    C. 35
    D. 45

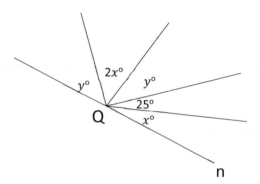

35) The perimeter of the trapezoid below is 36 cm. What is its area?

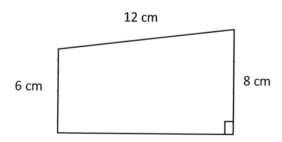

    A. 576 cm²

    B. 70 cm²

    C. 48 cm²

    D. 24 cm²

36) If 150 % of a number is 75, then what is the 90 % of that number?

    A. 45

    B. 50

    C. 70

    D.85

37) Triangle ABC is similar to triangle ADE

    A. 4

    B. 9

    C. 18

    D. 4.5

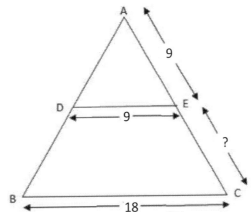

38) A football team had $20,000 to spend on supplies. The team spent $14,000 on new balls. New sport shoes cost $120 each. Which of the following inequalities represent the number of new shoes the team can purchase.

    A. $120x + 14,000 \leq 20,000$

    B. $120x + 14,000 \geq 20,000$

    C. $14,000x + 120 \leq 20,000$

    D. $14,000x + 12,0 \geq 20,000$

39) A card is drawn at random from a standard 52–card deck, what is the probability that the card is of Hearts? (The deck includes 13 of each suit clubs, diamonds, hearts, and spades)

    A. $\dfrac{1}{3}$

    B. $\dfrac{1}{4}$

    C. $\dfrac{1}{6}$

    D. $\dfrac{1}{52}$

40) The average of five numbers is 24. If a sixth number that is greater than 42 is added, then, which of the following could be the new average? (Select one or more answer choices)

    A. 25

    B. 26

    C. 27

    D. 28

41) Ella (E) is 4 years older than her friend Ava (A) who is 3 years younger than her sister Sofia (S). If E, A and S denote their ages, which one of the following represents the given information?

    A. $\begin{cases} E = A + 4 \\ S = A - 3 \end{cases}$

    B. $\begin{cases} E = A + 4 \\ A = S + 3 \end{cases}$

    C. $\begin{cases} A = E + 4 \\ S = A - 3 \end{cases}$

    D. $\begin{cases} E = A + 4 \\ A = S - 3 \end{cases}$

42) The length of a rectangle is 3 meters greater than 4 times its width. The perimeter of the rectangle is 36 meters. What is the area of the rectangle in meters?

    A. 35
    B. 45
    C. 55
    D. 65

43) The ratio of boys and girls in a class is 4:7. If there are 44 students in the class, how many more boys should be enrolled to make the ratio 1:1?

    A. 8

    B. 10

    C. 12

    D. 14

44) Mr. Jones saves $2,500 out of his monthly family income of $55,000. What fractional part of his income does he save?

A. $\dfrac{1}{22}$

B. $\dfrac{1}{11}$

C. $\dfrac{3}{25}$

D. $\dfrac{2}{15}$

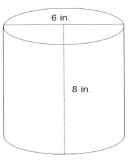

45) Jason needs an 75% average in his writing class to pass. On his first 4 exams, he earned scores of 68%, 72%, 85%, and 90%. What is the minimum score Jason can earn on his fifth and final test to pass?

A. 375
B. 315
C. 90
D. 60

46) What is the value of x in the following equation?

$$\frac{2}{3}x + \frac{1}{6} = \frac{1}{3}$$

A. 6

B. $\dfrac{1}{2}$

C. $\dfrac{1}{3}$

D. $\dfrac{1}{4}$

47) What is the surface area of the cylinder below?

    A. 48 π in²

    B. 57 π in²

    C. 66 π in²

    D. 288 π in²

48) The square of a number is $\frac{25}{64}$. What is the cube of that number?

    A. $\frac{5}{8}$

    B. $\frac{25}{254}$

    C. $\frac{125}{512}$

    D. $\frac{125}{64}$

49) What is the median of these numbers? 2, 27, 28, 19, 67, 44, 35

    A. 19

    B. 28

    C. 44

    D. 35

50) Right triangle ABC has two legs of lengths 6 cm (AB) and 8 cm (AC). What is the length of the third side (BC)?

    A. 4 cm

    B. 6 cm

    C. 8 cm

    D. 10 cm

51) What is the equivalent temperature of 104°F in Celsius?

$$C = \frac{5}{9} (F - 32)$$

    A. 32

    B. 40

    C. 48

    D. 52

52) If 40% of a number is 4, what is the number?

    A. 4

    B. 8

    C. 10

    D. 12

53) The circle graph below shows all Mr. Green's expenses for last month. If he spent $660 on his car, how much did he spend for his rent?

    A. $700

    B. $740

    C. $780

    D. $810

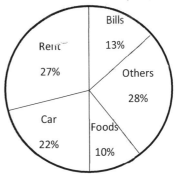

Mr. Green's monthly expenses

54) Jason is 9 miles ahead of Joe running at 5.5 miles per hour and Joe is running at the speed of 7 miles per hour. How long does it take Joe to catch Jason?

    A. 3 hours

    B. 4 hours

    C. 6 hours

    D. 8 hours

55) 55 students took an exam and 11 of them failed. What percent of the students passed the exam?

    A. 20%

    B. 40%

    C. 60%

    D. 80%

56) A bank is offering 3.5% simple interest on a savings account. If you deposit $12,000, how much interest will you earn in two years?

    A. $420

    B. $840

    C. $4200

    D. $8400

57) What is the area of the shaded region if the diameter of the bigger circle is 12 inches and the diameter of the smaller circle is 8 inches.

    A. 16π inch^2
    B. 20π inch^2
    C. 36π inch^2
    D. 80π inch^2

IF YOU FINISH BEFORE TIME IS CALLED, YOU MAY CHECK YOUR WORK ON THIS TEST.   **STOP**

SHSAT Mathematics Practice Tests Answers and Explanations

❋ Now, it's time to review your results to see where you went wrong and what areas you need to improve!

SHSAT Mathematics Practice Tests Answer Key													
SHSAT Practice Test 1							**SHSAT Practice Test 2**						
1	**67**	16	D	31	B	46	B	1	**64**	16	D	31	B	46	D
2	**1/2**	17	B	32	C	47	C	2	**9**	17	C	32	B	47	C
3	**2**	18	D	33	C	48	B	3	**2.25**	18	B	33	D	48	C
4	**33**	19	C	34	C	49	D	4	**42**	19	C	34	B	49	B
5	**16**	20	A	35	D	50	C	5	**175**	20	A	35	B	50	D
6	**C**	21	A	36	C	51	C	6	**B**	21	C	36	A	51	B
7	**A**	22	C	37	B	52	C	7	**D**	22	A	37	B	52	C
8	**C**	23	D	38	B	53	B	8	**A**	23	D	38	A	53	D
9	**B**	24	A	39	D	54	C	9	**C**	24	A	39	B	54	C
10	**C**	25	B	40	C	55	B	10	**A**	25	D	40	D	55	D
11	**D**	26	D	41	B	56	D	11	**A**	26	C	41	D	56	B
12	**C**	27	D	42	C	57	A	12	**D**	27	D	42	B	57	B
13	**C**	28	C	43	B			13	**B**	28	B	43	C	
14	**D**	29	D	44	B			14	**C**	29	D	44	A	
15	**C**	30	B	45	D			15	**D**	30	B	45	D	

SHSAT Mathematics Practice Test 1

Answers and Explanations

1) The answer is 67

$\alpha = 180° - 112° = 68°$

$\beta = 180° - 135° = 45°$

$x + \alpha + \beta = 180° \rightarrow x = 180° - 68° - 45° = 67°$

2) The answer is $\frac{1}{2}$

$AB = 12$ And $AC = 5$

$BC = \sqrt{12^2 + 5^2} = \sqrt{144 + 25} = \sqrt{169} = 13$

Perimeter $= 5 + 12 + 13 = 30$

Area $= \frac{5 \times 12}{2} = 5 \times 6 = 30$

In this case, the ratio of the perimeter of the triangle to its area is: $\frac{30}{30} = 1$

If the sides AB and AC become twice longer, then:

$AB = 24$ And $AC = 10$

$BC = \sqrt{24^2 + 10^2} = \sqrt{576 + 100} = \sqrt{676} = 26$

Perimeter $= 26 + 24 + 10 = 60$

Area $= \frac{10 \times 24}{2} = 10 \times 12 = 120$

In this case the ratio of the perimeter of the triangle to its area is: $\frac{60}{120} = \frac{1}{2}$

3) The answer is 2

Use PEMDAS (order of operation):

$$-18 + 6 \times (-5) - [4 + 22 \times (-4)] \div 2 + 8 = -18 - 30 - [4 - 88] \div 2 + 8$$
$$= -48 - [-84] \div 2 + 8 = -48 + 84 \div 2 + 8 = -48 + 42 + 8 = 2$$

4) The answer is 33

Since $N = 6$, substitute 6 for N in the equation $\frac{x-3}{5} = N$, which gives $\frac{x-3}{5} = 6$.
Multiplying both sides of $\frac{x-3}{5} = 6$ by 5 gives $x - 3 = 30$ and then adding 3 to both sides of

$x - 3 = 30$ then, $x = 33$.

5) The answer is 16

The rate of construction company$= \frac{30 \text{ cm}}{1 \text{ min}} = 30 \text{ cm/min}$

Height of the wall after 40 minutes $= \frac{30 \text{ cm}}{1 \text{ min}} \times 40 \text{ min} = 1200 \text{ cm}$

Let x be the height of wall, then $\frac{3}{4}x = 1200 \text{ cm} \rightarrow x = \frac{4 \times 1200}{3} \rightarrow x = 1600 \text{ cm} = 16 \, m$

6) Choice C is correct

Let x be the number. Write the equation and solve for x.

$(24 - x) \div x = 3$

Multiply both sides by x.

$(24 - x) = 3x$, then add x both sides. $24 = 4x$, now divide both sides by 4.

$x = 6$

7) Choice A is correct

The sum of supplement angles is 180. Let x be that angle. Therefore,

$x + 9x = 180$

$10x = 180$, divide both sides by 10: $x = 18$

8) Choice C is correct

The average speed of john is: $150 \div 6 = 25 \, km$

The average speed of Alice is: $180 \div 4 = 45 \, km$

Write the ratio and simplify. $25 : 45 \Rightarrow 5 : 9$

9) Choice B is correct

Since, E is the midpoint of AB, then the area of all triangles DAE, DEF, CFE and CBE are equal. Let x be the area of one of the triangle, Then: $4x = 100 \rightarrow x = 25$

The area of DEC $= 2x = 2(25) = 50$

10) Choice C is correct

$\$9 \times 10 = \$90$,   Petrol use: $10 \times 2 = 20$ liters

Petrol cost: $20 \times \$1 = \$20$

Money earned: $\$90 - \$20 = \$70$

11) Choice D is correct

Let x be the number of purple marbles. Let's review the choices provided:

A. $\frac{1}{10}$, if the probability of choosing a purple marble is one out of ten, then:

$$Probability = \frac{number\ of\ desired\ outcomes}{number\ of\ total\ outcomes} = \frac{x}{20 + 30 + 40 + x} = \frac{1}{10}$$

Use cross multiplication and solve for x. $10x = 90 + x \to 9x = 90 \to x = 9$

Since, number of purple marbles can be 9, then, choice be the probability of randomly selecting a purple marble from the bag.

Use same method for other choices.

B. $\frac{1}{4}$

$$\frac{x}{20 + 30 + 40 + x} = \frac{1}{4} \to 4x = 90 + x \to 3x = 90 \to x = 30$$

C. $\frac{2}{5}$

$$\frac{x}{20 + 30 + 40 + x} = \frac{2}{5} \to 5x = 180 + 2x \to 3x = 180 \to x = 60$$

D. $\frac{7}{15}$

$$\frac{x}{20 + 30 + 40 + x} = \frac{7}{15} \to 15x = 630 + 7x \to 8x = 630 \to x = 78.75$$

Number of purple marbles cannot be a decimal.

12) Choice C is correct

average = $\frac{sum\ of\ terms}{number\ of\ terms} = \frac{17 + 13 + 7 + 21 + 22}{5} = \frac{80}{5} = 16$

13) Choice C is correct

The smallest number is -15. To find the largest possible value of one of the other five integers, we need to choose the smallest possible integers for four of them. Let x be the largest number. Then: $-70 = (-15) + (-14) + (-13) + (-12) + (-11) + x \to -70 = -65 + x \to x = -70 + 65 = -5$

14) Choice D is correct.

$3x - 5 = 8.5 \to 3x = 8.5 + 5 = 13.5 \to x = \frac{13.5}{3} = 4.5$

Then; $5x + 3 = 5 (4.5) + 3 = 22.5 + 3 = 25.5$

15) Choice C is correct

Let x be the original price.

If the price of the sofa is decreased by 15% to \$476, then: $85\%\ of\ x = 476 \Rightarrow 0.85x = 476$ $\Rightarrow x = 476 \div 0.85 = 560$

16) Choice D is correct

Use Pythagorean Theorem: $a^2 + b^2 = c^2$

$9^2 + 12^2 = c^2 \Rightarrow 81 + 144 = c^2 \Rightarrow 225 = c^2 \Rightarrow c = 15$

17) Choice B is correct

Ratio of women to men in city A: $\dfrac{570}{600} = 0.95$

Ratio of women to men in city B: $\dfrac{291}{300} = 0.97$

Ratio of women to men in city C: $\dfrac{665}{700} = 0.95$

Ratio of women to men in city D: $\dfrac{528}{550} = 0.96$

18) Choice D is correct

Percentage of men in city A $= \dfrac{600}{1170} \times 100 = 51.28\%$

Percentage of women in city C $= \dfrac{665}{1365} \times 100 = 48.72\%$

Percentage of men in city A to percentage of women in city C $= \dfrac{51.28}{48.72} = 1.05$

19) Choice C is correct

Let the number of women should be added to city D be x, then:

$$\dfrac{528 + x}{550} = 1.2 \rightarrow 528 + x = 550 \times 1.2 = 660 \rightarrow x = 132$$

20) Choice A is correct

The percent of girls playing tennis is: 40% × 25% = 0.40 × 0.25 = 0.10 = 10%

21) Choice A is correct

Area of the circle is less than 16 π. Use the formula of areas of circles.

$$Area = \pi r^2 \Rightarrow 64\,\pi > \pi r^2 \Rightarrow 64 > r^2 \Rightarrow r < 8$$

Radius of the circle is less than 8. Let's put 8 for the radius. Now, use the circumference formula: $Circumference = 2\pi r = 2\pi\,(8) = 16\,\pi$

Since the radius of the circle is less than 8. Then, the circumference of the circle must be less than 16 π. Only choice A is less than 16 π.

22) Choice C is correct

$$\begin{cases} x + 4y = 10 \\ 5x + 10y = 20 \end{cases} \rightarrow \quad \text{Multiply the top equation by } -5 \text{ then,}$$

$$\begin{cases} -5x - 20y = -50 \\ 5x + 10y = 20 \end{cases} \rightarrow \quad \text{Add two equations}$$

$-10y = -30 \rightarrow y = 3$, plug in the value of y into the first equation

$$x + 4y = 10 \rightarrow x + 4(3) = 10 \rightarrow x + 12 = 10$$

Subtract 12 from both sides of the equation. Then: $x + 12 = 10 \rightarrow x = -2$

23) Choice D is correct

Write the equation and solve for B:

$0.60\ A = 0.20\ B$, divide both sides by 0.20, then:

$0.60/0.20\ A = B$, therefore:

$B = 3A$, and B is 3 times of A or it's 300% of A.

24) Choice A is correct

The length of MN is equal to: $\qquad 3x + 5x = 8x$

Then: $\qquad 8x = 40 \rightarrow x = \dfrac{40}{8} = 5$

The length of ON is equal to: $\qquad 5x = 5 \times 5 = 25$ cm

25) Choice B is correct

Use this formula: Percent of Change

$$\dfrac{\text{New Value} - \text{Old Value}}{\text{Old Value}} \times 100\%$$

$$\dfrac{16000 - 2000}{20000} \times 100\% = 20\% \text{ and } \dfrac{12800 - 1600}{16000} \times 100\% = 20\%$$

26) Choice D is correct

If the length of the box is 27, then the width of the box is one third of it, 9, and the height of the box is 3 (one third of the width). The volume of the box is:

$V = lwh = (27)(9)(3) = 729$

27) Choice D is correct

To find the number of possible outfit combinations, multiply number of options for each factor: $6 \times 3 \times 5 = 90$

28) Choice C is correct

Use simple interest formula: $I = prt$

$(I = interest, \quad p = principal, \quad r = rate, \quad t = time)$

$$I = (8,000)(0.045)(5) = 1,800$$

29) Choice D is correct

Of the 30 employees, there are 5 females under age 45 and 6 males age 45 or older. Therefore, the probability that the person selected will be either a female under age 45 or a male age 45 or older is: $\frac{5}{30} + \frac{6}{30} = \frac{11}{30}$

30) Choice B is correct

Plug in the value of $x = 30$ into both equations. Then:

$C(x) = x^2 + 2x = (30)^2 + 2(30) = 900 + 60 = 960$

$R(x) = 40x = 40 \times 30 = 1,200$

$1,200 - 960 = 240$

31) Choice B is correct

Two triangles ΔBAE and ΔBCD are similar. Then:

$$\frac{AE}{CD} = \frac{AB}{BC} \rightarrow \frac{4}{6} = \frac{x}{12} \rightarrow 48 - 4x = 6x \rightarrow 10x = 48 \rightarrow x = 4.8$$

32) Choice C is correct

The area of the trapezoid is:

$$Area = \frac{1}{2}h(b_1 + b_2) = \frac{1}{2}(x)(13 + 8) = 126$$

$$\rightarrow 10.5x = 126 \rightarrow x = 12$$

$y = \sqrt{5^2 + 12^2} = \sqrt{25 + 144} = \sqrt{169} = 13$

The perimeter of the trapezoid is: $\quad 12 + 13 + 8 + 13 = 46$

33) Choice C is correct

Add the first 5 numbers. 40 + 45 + 50 + 35 + 55 = 225

To find the distance traveled in the next 5 hours, multiply the average by number of hours.

Distance = Average × Rate = 50 × 5 = 250

Add both numbers.

250 + 225 = 475

34) Choice C is correct

Use distance formula:

Distance = Rate × time ⇒ 420 = 50 × T, divide both sides by 50. 420 / 50 = T ⇒ T = 8.4 hours.

Change hours to minutes for the decimal part. 0.4 hours = 0.4 × 60 = 24 minutes.

35) Choice D is correct

First calculate the number of feet that 1 inch represents:

100 ft ÷ 5 in = 20 ft/in

Then multiply this by the total number of inches:

18 in × 20 ft/in = 360 ft

36) Choice C is correct

Let x be the number. Write the equation and solve for x.

$\frac{2}{3} \times 18 = \frac{2}{5} \cdot x \Rightarrow \frac{2 \times 18}{3} = \frac{2x}{5}$, use cross multiplication to solve for x.

$5 \times 36 = 2x \times 3 \Rightarrow 180 = 6x \Rightarrow x = 30$

37) Choice B is correct

To find the discount, multiply the number by (100% − rate of discount).

Therefore, for the first discount we get: (D) (100% − 20%) = (D) (0.80) = 0.80 D

For increase of 10 %: (0.85 D) (100% + 10%) = (0.85 D) (1.10) = 0.88 D = 88% of D

38) Choice B is correct

Use the formula for Percent of Change

$$\frac{New\ Value - Old\ Value}{Old\ Value} \times 100\%$$

$\frac{28-40}{40} \times 100\% = -30\%$ (Negative sign here means that the new price is less than old price).

39) Choices D is correct

Some of prime numbers are: 2, 3, 5, 7, 11, 13

Find the product of two consecutive prime numbers:

2 × 3 = 6 (not in the options)

3 × 5 = 15 (bingo!)

5 × 7 = 35 (not in the options)

7 × 11 = 77 (not in the options)

40) Choice C is correct

Let's compare each fraction:

$\frac{2}{7} < \frac{3}{8} < \frac{5}{11} < \frac{3}{4}$

Only choice C provides the right order.

41) Choice B is correct

Use the information provided in the question to draw the shape.

Use Pythagorean Theorem: $a^2 + b^2 = c^2$

$40^2 + 30^2 = c^2 \Rightarrow 1600 + 900 = c^2 \Rightarrow 2500 = c^2 \Rightarrow c = 50$

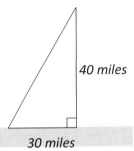

40 miles

42) Choice C is correct

30 miles

The ratio of boy to girls is 4:7. Therefore, there are 4 boys out of 11 students. To find the answer, first divide the total number of students by 11, then multiply the result by 4.

$44 \div 11 = 4 \Rightarrow 4 \times 4 = 16$

There are 16 boys and 28 (44 − 16) girls. So, 12 more boys should be enrolled to make the ratio 1:1

43) Choice B is correct

The question is this: 530.40 is what percent of 624?

Use percent formula:

$\text{part} = \frac{\text{percent}}{100} \times \text{whole}$, $530.40 = \frac{\text{percent}}{100} \times 624 \Rightarrow 530.40 = \frac{\text{percent} \times 624}{100}$
$\Rightarrow 53040 = \text{percent} \times 624 \Rightarrow$
$\text{percent} = \frac{53040}{624} = 85$

530.40 is 85 % of 624. Therefore, the discount is: $100\% - 85\% = 15\%$

44) Choice B is correct

If the score of Mia was 60, therefore the score of Ava is 30. Since, the score of Emma was half as that of Ava, therefore, the score of Emma is 15.

45) Choice D is correct

If 17 balls are removed from the bag at random, there will be one ball in the bag.

The probability of choosing a brown ball is 1 out of 18. Therefore, the probability of not choosing a brown ball is 17 out of 18 and the probability of having not a brown ball after removing 17 balls is the same.

46) Choice B is correct

Let x be the smallest number. Then, these are the numbers:

$x, x + 1, x + 2, x + 3, x + 4$

average $= \frac{\text{sum of terms}}{\text{number of terms}} \Rightarrow 38 = \frac{x+(x+1)+(x+2)+(x+3)+(x+4)}{5} \Rightarrow 38 = \frac{5x+10}{5} \Rightarrow 190 = 5x + 10$
$\Rightarrow 180 = 5x \Rightarrow x = 36$

47) Choice C is correct

The area of the floor is: 6 cm × 24 cm = 144 cm²

The number of tiles needed = 144 ÷ 8 = 18

48) Choice B is correct

$average\ (mean) = \frac{\text{sum of terms}}{\text{number of terms}} = \frac{9+12+15+16+19+16+1\ .5}{7} = 14.5$

49) Choice D is correct

If each book weighs $\frac{1}{5}$ pound, then 1 pound = 5 books. To find the number of books in 50 pounds, simply multiply this 5 by 50:

$50 \times 5 = 250$

50) Choice C is correct

The weight of 12.2 meters of this rope is: $12.2 \times 600\ g = 7,320\ g$

1 kg = 1,000 g, therefore, $7,320\ g \div 1000 = 7.32\ kg$

51) Choice C is correct

4% of the volume of the solution is alcohol. Let x be the volume of the solution.

Then: $4\%\ of\ x = 24\ ml \Rightarrow 0.04\ x = 24 \Rightarrow x = 24 \div 0.04 = 600$

52) Choice C is correct

Use the volume of square pyramid formula.

$V = \frac{1}{3}a^2h \Rightarrow V = \frac{1}{3}(12m)^2 \times 10m \Rightarrow V = 480\ m^3$

53) Choice B is correct

average $= \frac{\text{sum of terms}}{\text{number of terms}}$

The sum of the weight of all girls is: $18 \times 60 = 1080 \ kg$

The sum of the weight of all boys is: $32 \times 62 = 1984 \ kg$

The sum of the weight of all students is: $1080 + 1984 = 3064 \ kg$

$\text{average} = \dfrac{3064}{50} = 61.28$

54) Choice C is correct

Let x be the original price.

If the price of a laptop is decreased by 10% to $360, then:

$90 \ \% \ of \ x = 360 \Rightarrow 0.90x = 360 \Rightarrow x = 360 \div 0.90 = 400$

55) Choice B is correct

Write the numbers in order: 4, 5, 8, 9, 13, 15, 18

Since we have 7 numbers (7 is odd), then the median is the number in the middle, which is 9.

56) Choice D is correct

Formula for the Surface area of a cylinder is:

$$SA = 2\pi r^2 + 2\pi rh \rightarrow 150\pi = 2\pi r^2 + 2\pi r(10) \rightarrow r^2 + 10r - 75 = 0$$

$$(r + 15)(r - 5) = 0 \rightarrow r = 5 \quad or \quad r = -15 \ (unacceptable)$$

57) Choice A is correct

Let x be the number of years. Therefore, $2,000 per year equals $2000x$.

starting from $24,000 annual salary means you should add that amount to $2000x$.

Income more than that is:

$I > 2000x + 24000$

SHSAT Mathematics Practice Test 2

Answers and Explanations

1) The answer is 64

The area of the circle is 16π cm^2, then, its diameter is 8cm.

$$area\ of\ a\ circle = \pi r^2 = 16\pi \rightarrow r^2 = 16 \rightarrow r = 4$$

Radius of the circle is 4 and diameter is twice of it, 8.

One side of the square equals to the diameter of the circle. Then:

$$Area\ of\ square = side \times side = 8 \times 8 = 64$$

2) The answer is 9

The median of a set of data is the value located in the middle of the data set. Combine the 2 sets provided, and organize them in ascending order:

{1, 3, 4, 6, 8, 10, 12, 14, 15, 17}

Since there are an even number of items in the resulting list, the median is the average of the two middle numbers.

$$Median = (8 + 10) \div 2 = 9$$

3) The answer is 2.25

Write a proportion and solve for the missing number.

$\frac{32}{12} = \frac{6}{x} \rightarrow 32x = 6 \times 12 = 72$

$$32x = 72 \rightarrow x = \frac{72}{32} = 2.25$$

4) The answer is 42

Plug in the value of x and y. $3(x - 2y) + (2 - x)^2$ when $x = 5$ and $y = -3$

$x = 5$ and $y = -3$

$$3(x - 2y) + (2 - x)^2 = 3(5 - 2(-3)) + (2 - 5)^2 = 3(5 + 6) + (-3)^2 = 33 + 9 = 42$$

5) The answer is 175

$-60 = 115 - x$, First, subtract 115 from both sides of the equation. Then:
$-60 - 115 = 115 - 115 - x \rightarrow -175 = -x$

Multiply both sides by (-1): $\rightarrow x = 175$

6) Choice B is correct

The area of the non-shaded region is equal to the area of the bigger rectangle subtracted by the area of smaller rectangle.

Area of the bigger rectangle = 12 × 16 = 192

Area of the smaller rectangle = 10 × 4 = 40

Area of the non-shaded region = 192 − 40 = 152

7) Choice D is correct

In the figure angle A is labeled $(3x − 2)$ and it measures 37. Thus, $3x − 2 = 37$ and $3x = 39$ or $x = 13$.

That means that angle B, which is labeled $(5x)$, must measure $5 × 13 = 65$.

Since the three angles of a triangle must add up to 180,

$$37 + 65 + y − 8 = 180, \text{ then: } y + 94 = 108 \rightarrow y = 180 − 94 = 86$$

8) Choice A is correct

Simplify and combine like terms.

$$(6x^3 − 8x^2 + 2x^4) − (4x^2 − 2x^4 + 2x^3) \Rightarrow (6x^3 − 8x^2 + 2x^4) − 4x^2 + 2x^4 − 2x^3 \Rightarrow$$
$$4x^4 + 4x^3 − 12x^2$$

9) Choice C is correct

Let's find the mean (average), mode and median of the number of cities for each type of pollution.

Number of cities for each type of pollution: 6, 3, 4, 9, 8

$$average \ (mean) = \frac{sum \ of \ terms}{number \ of \ terms} = \frac{6+3+4+9+8}{5} = \frac{30}{5} = 6$$

Median is the number in the middle. To find median, first list numbers in order from smallest to largest.

3, 4, 6, 8, 9

Median of the data is 6.

Mode is the number which appears most often in a set of numbers. Therefore, there is no mode in the set of numbers.

Median = Mean, then, $a=c$

10) Choice A is correct

Percent of cities in the type of pollution A: $\frac{6}{10} \times 100 = 60\%$

Percent of cities in the type of pollution C: $\frac{4}{10} \times 100 = 40\%$

Percent of cities in the type of pollution E: $\frac{9}{10} \times 100 = 90\%$

11) Choice A is correct

Let the number of cities should be added to type of pollutions B be x. Then:

$$\frac{x+3}{8} = 0.625 \rightarrow x + 3 = 8 \times 0.625 \rightarrow x + 3 = 5 \rightarrow x = 2$$

12) Choice D is correct

let x be total number of cards in the box, then number of red cards is: $x - 246$

The probability of choosing a red card is one third. Then:

$$probability = \frac{1}{3} = \frac{x-132}{x}$$

Use cross multiplication to solve for x.

$$x \times 1 = 3(x - 246) \rightarrow x = 3x - 738 \rightarrow 2x = 738 \rightarrow x = 369$$

13) Choice B is correct

Subtract $\frac{1}{6b}$ and $\frac{1}{b^2}$ from both sides of the equation. Then:

$$\frac{1}{6b^2} + \frac{1}{6b} = \frac{1}{b^2} \rightarrow \frac{1}{6b^2} - \frac{1}{b^2} = -\frac{1}{6b}$$

Multiply both numerator and denominator of the fraction $\frac{1}{b^2}$ by 6. Then:

$$\frac{1}{6b^2} - \frac{6}{6b^2} = -\frac{1}{6b}$$

Simplify the first side of the equation: $-\frac{5}{6b^2} = -\frac{1}{6b}$

Use cross multiplication method: $30b = 6b^2 \rightarrow 30 = 6b \rightarrow b = 5$

14) Choice C is correct

The population is increased by 15% and 20%. 15% increase changes the population to 115% of original population.

For the second increase, multiply the result by 120%.

$(1.15) \times (1.20) = 1.38 = 138\%$

38 percent of the population is increased after two years.

15) Choice D is correct

Solve for x.

$-2 \leq 2x - 4 < 8 \Rightarrow$ (add 4 all sides) $-2 + 4 \leq 2x - 4 + 4 < 8 + 4 \Rightarrow$

$2 \leq 2x < 12 \Rightarrow$ (divide all sides by 2) $1 \leq x < 6$

x is between 1 and 6. Choice D represent this inequality.

16) Choice D is correct

$Volume\ of\ a\ box = length \times width \times height = 4 \times 5 \times 6 = 120$

17) Choice C is correct

y is the intersection of the three circles. Therefore, it must be odd (from circle A), negative (from circle B), and multiple of 5 (from circle C).

From the options, only -5 is odd, negative and multiple of 5.

18) Choice B is correct

Recall that the formula for the average is:

Average= $\dfrac{sum\ of\ data}{number\ of\ data}$

First, compute the total weight of all balls in the basket:

25 g = $\dfrac{total\ weigh}{20\ balls}$

25g × 20 = total weight = 500 g

Next, find the total weight of the 5 largest marbles:

40 g = $\dfrac{total\ weigh}{5\ marbles}$

40 g × 5 = total weight = 200 g

The total weight of the heaviest balls is 200 g. Then, the total weight of the remaining 15 balls is 300 g. 500 g – 200 g = 300 g.

The average weight of the remaining balls:

Average = $\dfrac{300\ g}{15\ marbles}$ = 20 g per ball

19) Choice C is correct

To find the number of possible outfit combinations, multiply number of options for each factor:

$3 \times 5 \times 4 = 60$

20) Choice A is correct

In the stadium the ratio of home fans to visiting fans in a crowd is 5:7. Therefore, total number of fans must be divisible by 12: 5 + 7 = 12.
Let's review the choices:
A. 12,324: $12,324 \div 12 = 1,027$

B. 42,326 $42,326 \div 12 = 3,527.166$

C. 44,566 $44,566 \div 12 = 3,713.833$

D. 66,812 $66,812 \div 12 = 5,567.666$

Only choice A when divided by 12 results a whole number.

21) Choice C is correct

Three times of 24,000 is 72,000. One sixth of them cancelled their tickets.

One sixth of 72,000 equals 12,000 ($\frac{1}{6} \times 72000 = 12000$).

60,000(72,000 – 12,000 = 60,000) fans are attending this week

22) Choice A is correct

The area of the square is 595.36. Therefore, the side of the square is square root of the area.

$\sqrt{595.36} = 24.4$

Four times the side of the square is the perimeter:

$4 \times 24.4 = 97.6$

23) Choice D is correct

$$2\frac{2}{3} - 1\frac{5}{6} = 2\frac{4}{6} - 1\frac{5}{6} = \frac{16}{6} - \frac{11}{6} = \frac{5}{6}$$

24) Choice A is correct

The width of the rectangle is twice its length. Let x be the length. Then, $width = 2x$

Perimeter of the rectangle is 2 (width + length) = $2(2x + x) = 60 \Rightarrow 6x = 60 \Rightarrow x = 10$

Length of the rectangle is 10 meters.

25) Choice D is correct

Change the numbers to decimal and then compare.

$\frac{2}{3} = 0.666\ldots$

0.68

$67\% = 0.67$

$\frac{4}{5} = 0.80$

Then:

$$\frac{2}{3} < 67\% < 0.68 < \frac{4}{5}$$

26) Choice C is correct

$$\text{average (mean)} = \frac{\text{sum of terms}}{\text{number of terms}} \Rightarrow 88 = \frac{\text{sum of terms}}{50} \Rightarrow sum = 88 \times 50 = 4400$$

The difference of 94 and 69 is 25. Therefore, 25 should be subtracted from the sum.

$4400 - 25 = 4375$

$$\text{mean} = \frac{\text{sum of terms}}{\text{number of terms}} \Rightarrow \text{mean} = \frac{4375}{50} = 87.5$$

27) Choice D is correct

Let x be the number of current stamps in the collection. Then:

$$\frac{6}{5}x - x = 100 \rightarrow \frac{1}{5}x = 100 \rightarrow x = 500$$

50% more of 500 is: 500 + 0.50 × 500 = 500 + 250 = 750.

28) Choice B is correct

To get a sum of 6 for two dice, we can get 5 different options:

(5, 1), (4, 2), (3, 3), (2, 4), (1, 5)

To get a sum of 9 for two dice, we can get 4 different options:

(6, 3), (5, 4), (4, 5), (3, 6)

Therefore, there are 9 options to get the sum of 6 or 9.

Since, we have 6 × 6 = 36 total options, the probability of getting a sum of 6 and 9 is 9 out of 36 or $\frac{1}{4}$.

29) Choice D is correct

Use formula of rectangle prism volume.

$$V = (length)(width)(height) \Rightarrow 2000 = (25)(10)(height) \Rightarrow$$

$$height = 2000 \div 250 = 8$$

30) Choice B is correct

The diagonal of the square is 8. Let x be the side.

Use Pythagorean Theorem: $a^2 + b^2 = c^2$

$$x^2 + x^2 = 8^2 \Rightarrow 2x^2 = 8^2 \Rightarrow 2x^2 = 64 \Rightarrow x^2 = 32 \Rightarrow x = \sqrt{32}$$

The area of the square is:

$$\sqrt{32} \times \sqrt{32} = 32$$

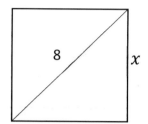

31) Choice B is correct

The sum of 8 numbers is greater than 240 and less than 320. Then, the average of the 8 numbers must be greater than 30 and less than 40.

$$\frac{240}{8} < x < \frac{320}{8}$$

$$30 < x < 40$$

The only choice that is between 30 and 40 is 35.

32) Choice B is correct

$$\text{Probability} = \frac{number\ of\ desired\ outcomes}{number\ of\ total\ outcomes} = \frac{18}{12+18+18+24} = \frac{18}{72} = \frac{1}{4}$$

33) Choice D is correct

$$\text{average} = \frac{\text{sum of terms}}{\text{number of terms}} \Rightarrow \text{(average of 6 numbers) } 12 = \frac{\text{sum of numbers}}{6} \Rightarrow \text{sum of 6}$$
numbers is 12 × 6 = 72

(average of 4 numbers) $10 = \dfrac{\text{sum of numbers}}{4} \Rightarrow$ sum of 4 numbers is 10 × 4 = 40

sum of 6 numbers − sum of 4 numbers = sum of 2 numbers 72 − 40 = 32

average of 2 numbers = $\dfrac{32}{2} = 16$

34) Choice B is correct

The angles on a straight line add up to 180 degrees. Then:

$x + 25 + y + 2x + y = 180$

Then, $3x + 2y = 180 - 25 \rightarrow 3(35) + 2y = 155$

$\rightarrow 2y = 155 - 105 = 50 \rightarrow y = 25$

35) Choice B is correct

The perimeter of the trapezoid is 36 cm.

Therefore, the missing side (height) is $= 36 - 8 - 12 - 6 = 10$

Area of a trapezoid: $A = \frac{1}{2}h\,(b_1 + b_2) = \frac{1}{2}(10)(6 + 8) = 70$

36) Choice A is correct

First, find the number.

Let x be the number. Write the equation and solve for x.

150 % of a number is 75, then:

$1.5 \times x = 75 \Rightarrow x = 75 \div 1.5 = 50$

90 % of 50 is: $0.9 \times 50 = 45$

37) Choice B is correct

If two triangles are similar, then the ratios of corresponding sides are equal.

$\frac{AC}{AE} = \frac{BC}{DE} = \frac{18}{9} = 2$

$\frac{AC}{AE} = 2$

This ratio can be used to find the length of AC: $AC = 2 \times AE$, $AC = 2 \times 9$

$AC = 18$

The length of AE is given as 9 and we now know the length of AC is 18, therefore:

$EC = AC - AE$

$EC = 18 - 9,\qquad EC = 9$

38) Choice A is correct

Let x be the number of new shoes the team can purchase. Therefore, the team can purchase $120\,x$.

The team had $20,000 and spent $14,000. Now the team can spend on new shoes $6,000 at most.

Now, write the inequality:

$120x + 14,000 \leq 20,000$

39) Choice B is correct

The probability of choosing a Hearts is $\frac{13}{52} = \frac{1}{4}$

40) Choice D is correct

First, find the sum of five numbers.

average = $\dfrac{\text{sum of terms}}{\text{number of terms}} \Rightarrow 24 = \dfrac{\text{sum of 5 numbers}}{5} \Rightarrow$ sum of 5 numbers = 24 × 5 = 120

The sum of 5 numbers is 120. If a sixth number that is greater than 42 is added to these numbers, then the sum of 6 numbers must be greater than 162.

120 + 42 = 162

If the number was 42, then the average of the numbers is:

average = $\dfrac{\text{sum of terms}}{\text{number of terms}} = \dfrac{162}{6} = 27$

Since the number is bigger than 42. Then, the average of six numbers must be greater than 27. Choice D is greater than 27.

41) Choice D is correct

$E = 4 + A$

$A = S - 3$

42) Choice B is correct

Let L be the length of the rectangular and W be the with of the rectangular. Then,

$$L = 4W + 3$$

The perimeter of the rectangle is 36 meters. Therefore: $2L + 2W = 36, \quad L + W = 18$

Replace the value of L from the first equation into the second equation and solve for W:

$$(4W + 3) + W = 18 \rightarrow 5W + 3 = 18 \rightarrow 5W = 15 \rightarrow W = 3$$

The width of the rectangle is 3 meters and its length is: $L = 4W + 3 = 4(3) + 3 = 15$

The area of the rectangle is: length × width = 3 × 15 = 45

43) Choice C is correct

Th ratio of boy to girls is 4:7. Therefore, there are 4 boys out of 11 students. To find the answer, first divide the total number of students by 11, then multiply the result by 4.

$44 \div 11 = 4 \Rightarrow 4 \times 4 = 16$

There are 16 boys and 28 (44 − 16) girls. So, 12 more boys should be enrolled to make the ratio 1:1

44) Choice A is correct

2,500 out of 55,000 equals to $\dfrac{2500}{55000} = \dfrac{25}{550} = \dfrac{1}{22}$

45) Choice D is correct

Jason needs an 75% average to pass for five exams. Therefore, the sum of 5 exams must be at lease $5 \times 75 = 375$

The sum of 4 exams is: $68 + 72 + 85 + 90 = 315$

The minimum score Jason can earn on his fifth and final test to pass is: $375 - 315 = 60$

46) Choice D is correct

Isolate and solve for x.

$\dfrac{2}{3}x + \dfrac{1}{6} = \dfrac{1}{3} \Rightarrow \dfrac{2}{3}x = \dfrac{1}{3} - \dfrac{1}{6} = \dfrac{1}{6} \Rightarrow \dfrac{2}{3}x = \dfrac{1}{6}$

Multiply both sides by the reciprocal of the coefficient of x.

$(\dfrac{3}{2})\dfrac{2}{3}x = \dfrac{1}{6}(\dfrac{3}{2}) \Rightarrow x = \dfrac{3}{12} = \dfrac{1}{4}$

47) Choice C is correct

Surface Area of a cylinder = 2πr (r + h),

The radius of the cylinder is 3 (6 ÷ 2) inches and its height is 8 inches. Therefore,

Surface Area of a cylinder = 2π (3) (3 + 8) = 66 π

48) Choice C is correct

The square of a number is $\dfrac{25}{64}$, then the number is the square root of $\dfrac{25}{64}$

$\sqrt{\dfrac{25}{64}} = \dfrac{5}{8}$

The cube of the number is: $(\dfrac{5}{8})^3 = \dfrac{125}{512}$

49) Choice B is correct

Write the numbers in order: 2, 19, 27, 28, 35, 44, 67

Median is the number in the middle. So, the median is 28.

50) Choice D is correct

Use Pythagorean Theorem: $a^2 + b^2 = c^2$

$6^2 + 8^2 = c^2 \Rightarrow 100 = c^2 \Rightarrow c = 10$

51) Choice B is correct

Plug in 104 for F and then solve for C.

$C = \frac{5}{9}(F - 32) \Rightarrow C = \frac{5}{9}(104 - 32) \Rightarrow C = \frac{5}{9}(72) = 40$

52) Choice C is correct

Let x be the number. Write the equation and solve for x.

$40\% \ of \ x = 4 \Rightarrow 0.40 \ x = 4 \Rightarrow x = 4 \div 0.40 = 10$

53) Choice D is correct

Let x be all expenses, then $\frac{22}{100}x = \$660 \rightarrow x = \frac{100 \times \$660}{22} = \$3,000$

He spent for his rent: $\frac{27}{100} \times \$3,000 = \$810$

54) Choice C is correct

The distance between Jason and Joe is 9 miles. Jason running at 5.5 miles per hour and Joe is running at the speed of 7 miles per hour. Therefore, every hour the distance is 1.5 miles less. $9 \div 1.5 = 6$

55) Choice D is correct

The failing rate is 11 out of 55 = $\frac{11}{55}$

Change the fraction to percent:

$\frac{11}{55} \times 100\% = 20\%$

20 percent of students failed. Therefore, 80 percent of students passed the exam.

56) Choice B is correct

Use simple interest formula:

$I = prt$

(I = interest, p = principal, r = rate, t = time)

$$I = (12000)(0.035)(2) = 840$$

57) Choice B is correct.

To find the area of the shaded region subtract smaller circle from bigger circle.

$S_{bigger} - S_{smaller} = \pi (r_{bigger})^2 - \pi (r_{smaller})^2 \Rightarrow S_{bigger} - S_{smaller} = \pi (6)^2 - \pi (4)^2$

$\Rightarrow 36\pi - 16\pi = 20\pi$

"Effortless Math Education" Publications

Effortless Math authors' team strives to prepare and publish the best quality SHSAT Mathematics learning resources to make learning Math easier for all. We hope that our publications help you learn Math in an effective way and prepare for the SHSAT test.

We all in Effortless Math wish you good luck and successful studies!

Effortless Math Authors

Visit www.EffortlessMath.com
for Online Math Practice

www.EffortlessMath.com

... So Much More Online!

✓ FREE Math lessons

✓ More Math learning books!

✓ Mathematics Worksheets

✓ Online Math Tutors

Need a PDF version of this book?

Visit www.EffortlessMath.com

Made in the USA
Middletown, DE
29 September 2020